MW00709375

MASTERING NEW YORK'S GRADE 4 ENGLISH LANGUAGE ARTS STANDARDS

JAMES KILLORAN

STUART ZIMMER

MARK JARRETT

JARRETT PUBLISHING COMPANY

EAST COAST OFFICE
P.O. Box 1460
Ronkonkoma, NY 11779
631-981-4248

WEST COAST OFFICE
10 Folin Lane
Lafayette, CA 94549
925-906-9742

1-800-859-7679   Fax: 631-588-4722
www.jarrettpub.com

This book includes material from many different sources. Occasionally it is not possible to determine if a particular source is copyrighted, and if so, who is the copyright owner. Every effort has been made to trace the ownership of all copyrighted material and to secure the necessary permissions to reprint these selections. If there has been a copyright infringement with any material in this book, it is unintentional. We extend our sincerest apologies and would be happy to make immediate and appropriate restitution upon proof of copyright ownership.

Grateful acknowledgment is made to the following to reprint the copyrighted materials listed below:

Alfred A. Knopf, Inc. for the poem, "Sea Calm" by Langston Hughes *in The Collected Poems of Langston Hughes*, edited by Arnold Rampersad, © 1994. Black Dog and Leventhal Publishers for "Alvin Ailey" by Andrea Davis Pinkney in *African-American Read Aloud Stories*, ©1998. *Boys Life Magazine* for "You're Alive," by Gail Skroback Hennessey, May, 1999 issue. Children's Better Health Institute for the articles in *Child Life*, "Happy Birthday, Basketball" by Charles Davis, March, 2000 issue; *Elizabeth Blackwell: The First Woman Doctor* in the April/May, 2000 issue. *Cobblestone Magazine* for the article, "School Days" by Joyce Haynes, February, 1999 issue. Curtis Brown, Ltd. for "Homework" by Jane Yolen in *Breakfast, Books, and Dreams* published by Frederick Warne, ©1981 by Jane Yolen. *Cricket Magazine* for the story, "Killer" by Sandy Fox, August, 1998 issue; for the article, "When Money Grew on Trees" by Amy Butler Greenfield, August, 2001 issue; for the stories, "The Devoted Son and the Thief" and "The Chest of Broken Glass," June, 1996 issue; for the article "Danger From the Sky" by Barbara Saffer, October, 1998 issue; for the story "Earth and Water and Sky" by Bryan A. Bushemi, October, 1998 issue; for the story "How Horses Communicate" by Dorothy Hinshaw Patent, August, 1998 issue. Dutton Children's Books for the stories "The Shoemaker and the Elves" and "How Big Mouth Wrestled the Giant" in *Diane Goode's Book of Giants and Little People*, © 1997. Follett Press for the poem, "City, City" by Marci Ridlon in *That Was Summer*, © 1969. Greenwillow Books for the story "The Wolf and the Dog" in *The Acorn Tree and Other Folktales*, © 1995. *Highlights For Children* for the story "Invention Number Three" by Jeanne DiPrau, November, 2002 issue; for the story, "Abby Takes Her Shot" by Susan Dyckman, January, 2001 issue; for the story, "The Recital" by Kathleen Bennere Duble, February, 1999 issue; for the story, "The Mystery of the Unfriendly Neighbor" by Diane Burns, September, 2001 issue; for the story, "Into the Cave" by Harriet Diller and Betty Hodges, July, 2005 issue; McGraw-Hill for "The Sandpiper," from *The Little Whistler* by Frances Frost. ©1949. *Odyssey Magazine*, for the article, "Batty About Bats!" by Kathian M. Kowalski, © 1999, Number 3 issue. Pleasant Company Publications for the novel *Josephina Learns A Lesson* by Valerie Tripp, © 1997. Random House for the poem, "The Library" by Barbara A. Huff in *The Random House Book of Poetry for Children*, selected and introduced by Jack Prelutsky, © 1983. Simon and Schuster for the story "The Emperor and the Peasant Boy," in *The Book of Virtues For Young People*, edited by William J. Bennett, © 1997. *Spider: The Magazine For Children* for, "Hard-Boiled Eggs" a tale from Hungary retold by Tom R. Kovach, March, 2003 issue.

NOTE: In some cases the previously published material has been adapted and edited to maintain a fourth grade readability level.

Copyright 2005 by Jarrett Publishing Company

All rights reserved. No part of this book may be reproduced in any form or by any means, including electronic, photographic, mechanical, or by any device for storage and retrieval of information, without the express written permission of the publisher. Requests for permission to copy any part of this book should be mailed to:

Jarrett Publishing Company
Post Office Box 1460
Ronkonkoma, New York 11779

ISBN 1-882422-88-0
Printed in the United States of America
First Edition
10 9 8 7 6 5 4 3 2 1   08 07 06 05

ACKNOWLEDGMENTS

The authors would like to thank the following educators who helped review the manuscript. Their comments, suggestions, and recommendations have proved invaluable in preparing this book.

Ms. Kathy Conway-Gervais
President of the Nassau Reading Council
Regional Director for the NYS Reading Association
Associate Professor, Long Island University and Touro College

Dr. Dorothy Troike
Professor, Literacy Department
State University of New York College at Cortland

Linda Smolen
Director of Reading, Buffalo Public Schools
Buffalo, New York

Cover design, layout, graphics, and typesetting: Burmar Technical Corporation, Albertson, N.Y.

This book is dedicated...

to my wife Donna, my children Christian, Carrie, and Jesse, and my grandson Aiden

— James Killoran

to my wife Joan, my children Todd and Ronald, and my grandchildren Katie and Jared

— Stuart Zimmer

to my first teachers, Beverly and Paul Jarrett

— Mark Jarrett

Other books by Killoran, Zimmer, and Jarrett

Mastering New York's Grade 4 English Language Arts Test
Mastering New York's Grade 8 English Language Arts Test
Mastering the TAKS Grade 4 in Reading and Writing
Mastering the TAKS Grade 3 in Reading
La Prepa: Dominando la prueba TAKS de lectura de tercer grado
Mastering the TAKS Grade 11 Exit Level ELA
Mastering the Grade 7 Writing TEKS
Mastering the Georgia Middle Grades Writing Assessment
Mastering the Grade 6 PSSA Writing Assessment
Mastering the Grade 5 PSSA Reading Test
Mastering the Grade 3 ISAT Reading and Writing Test
Mastering the Grade 5 ISAT Reading and Writing Test
Mastering the Grade 3 MCAS Reading Test
Mastering the Grade 4 MCAS Tests in English Language Arts
Mastering Ohio's Fourth Grade Proficiency Tests in Reading and Writing
Mastering the Grade 4 FCAT Reading and Writing Test
Excelling on the FCAT 10 in Reading
Introducing the Elementary English Language Arts

TABLE OF CONTENTS

INTRODUCTION

This year you will take an important test — **New York's Grade 4 English Language Arts Test.** This book will help you prepare for this test, as well as show you how to improve your reading and writing skills. This opening section introduces you to certain skills that will help you to become a better reader:

⭐ In the first chapter you will learn what good readers do to understand what they have read.

⭐ There are several types of selections you should be able to read in fourth grade. Chapter 2 looks at stories, including their setting, characters, and plot. It also looks at poems and their special features. Chapter 3 looks at informational readings, such as a magazine article. These provide information about a topic.

UNLAWFUL TO PHOTOCOPY

1

HOW TO BE A GOOD READER

Reading is a skill in which you connect words on a page with ideas and pictures in your head. Would you like to be a better reader? Recognizing words is just part of it. The most important thing is **understanding** the ideas of the writer and seeing how they fit in with your own ideas.

A good reader is an **active** reader. When you read, be sure to ask yourself questions. Think about how the author's ideas match up with your own. Thinking about what you read helps you to understand the reading better. In this chapter, you will learn some important ways of thinking about what you read.

READING STRATEGIES

A **strategy** is a plan for winning a battle or achieving a goal. Just as a general uses a strategy to win a battle, good readers use special strategies when they read. Experts in reading have identified several **strategies** used by good readers to better understand and apply what they read. These include things *before*, *during*, and *after* reading.

BEFORE READING

When you are about to read something, you should always ask yourself:

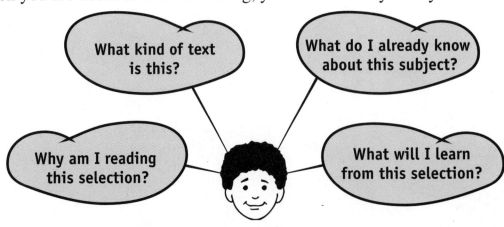

What kind of text is this?

What do I already know about this subject?

Why am I reading this selection?

What will I learn from this selection?

UNLAWFUL TO PHOTOCOPY

Think about *why* you are reading the selection. For example, are you reading to find out information or to enjoy a good story?

Next, look over the title and the passage as a whole to get a general idea of what the reading is about. See if there are illustrations, headings, or other clues about the subject of the reading. Then think about what you already know about this kind of reading and its subject. Finally, ask yourself what would you like to find out about that topic.

DURING READING

Good readers think actively while they read. You can do this by practicing the following strategies:

ASK QUESTIONS

As you read, ask yourself questions. Then look for the answers as they come up in the reading. For example, ask **where** and **when** the action takes place. Good readers ask **what** is happening in the reading. They also ask **why** things in the story happen the way they do. Asking yourself questions helps you to stay focused on what you are reading. It helps you to understand the reading better.

MAKE MENTAL PICTURES

Much of what we know about the world comes through our five senses. When you read, try to picture the things you are reading about. Close your eyes for just a moment. Pretend that you are watching the characters as they move about in the story, almost like a movie. Imagine what it would be like to see, smell, taste, or touch what each character is experiencing.

MAKE CONNECTIONS

Connect the reading to what you already know. As you read, ask yourself if each new thing you read about reminds you of anything you already know. This could be something that happened to you or that you have read or heard about. Compare the reading to what you already know.

Unlawful to Photocopy

THINK ABOUT WHAT IS IMPORTANT

As you read, focus on the author's *main ideas* or the *key events* in the story. Ask yourself which details are most important for understanding what the author has to say. The title is important because it often tells you what the selection is about. Many paragraphs will have **topic sentences** stating the main idea of the paragraph. If you are reading a story, think about the problems faced by the major characters and how they solve them.

MAKE PREDICTIONS

As you read, try to predict what will happen next. For example, if a character in a story faces a problem, think about some of the ways the problem could be solved. Then see if the character solved the problem using one of the ways you thought of. Even if your prediction is wrong, it helps you to understand the story better.

SUMMARIZE

When you read, you should pause every so often to think about what you have just read. Silently summarize what is important in the passage. To **summarize**, restate what the reading says in shorter form, using your own words. Make sure you understand what you are reading. Check any details you are not sure about before you read on.

BE A PROBLEM-SOLVER

If you have trouble understanding something, don't just continue reading. Take steps to figure it out. For example, re-read a difficult section to understand it better. Try to figure out the meaning of a difficult word by looking at surrounding words and sentences, or by looking the word up in a dictionary.

UNLAWFUL TO PHOTOCOPY

The following chart summarizes the methods used by good readers. See how many of these methods you can use when you read.

Ask Questions
Good readers ask themselves questions about what they are reading.

Make Connections
Good readers make connections with what they already know.

Think about What's Important
Good readers decide what is important.

Summarize
Good readers summarize what they are reading in their own words.

STRATEGIES USED BY GOOD READERS

Make Predictions
Good readers make predictions and draw conclusions.

Make Mental Pictures
Good readers picture what is happening in the selection.

Be a Problem-solver
When good readers cannot understand something, they take steps to figure it out.

UNLAWFUL TO PHOTOCOPY

AFTER READING

After you finish reading a selection, think about what you have just read. Think again about what was **most important** in the reading. Mentally **summarize** what the reading was about. Think about what you learned from the reading and how it fits in with what you know. Ask yourself the following:

★ What was the message or main idea of the reading?

★ Have I learned anything *new*?

★ What were some "memorable" words and phrases?

PRACTICE MODEL

Let's see how a good reader actually uses these methods. On the following page is a reading passage about the Native Americans of the Great Lakes. This model shows what a good reader thinks about *before, during,* and *after* reading.

BEFORE READING

Before reading, a good reader asks:

★ *Why am I reading this?*
I am reading this selection to find out about the Native American tribes who once lived around the Great Lakes.

★ *What do I already know about this subject?*
In school, I have studied some of the Native American tribes who once lived in New York State. I do not know anything about Native American tribes living around the Great Lakes. However, I know the Great Lakes are large freshwater lakes in the northern part of the United States.

UNLAWFUL TO PHOTOCOPY

DURING READING

Here are some things a good reader might think about while reading this article:

The Junior Encyclopedia

American Indian Tribes of the Great Lakes

The Great Lakes are five of the largest freshwater lakes in the world. They are located between the United States and Canada. Long before the voyages of Christopher Columbus, American Indian tribes lived in forests along the shores of the Great Lakes. Members of these tribes developed ways of life using the resources that nature made available to them.

MAKE CONNECTIONS
I know about freshwater lakes. This information helps me draw connections between the Indians and this kind of environment.

What other connections can you make from this first paragraph?

_____

_____

_____

MAKE PREDICTIONS
From the text, I can tell this is an article, not a story. It will tell me facts about the lifestyles of the Great Lakes tribes.

What other predictions would you make?

_____

_____

_____

CREATE MENTAL IMAGES
I can just imagine how the American Indian settlements looked, scattered in the forests around the Great Lakes.

What other mental pictures would you create?

_____

_____

_____

Most of the villages of the Great Lakes tribes were built near rivers or lakes. Canoes were used for transportation and to search for food. Usually, the men did the hunting, fishing, and making of canoes. They used natural materials, such as rocks and plant fibers, to make tools and weapons. They used spears, hooks, and nets to fish in the Great Lakes. Bows and arrows, spears and clubs were used to kill deer, rabbits, moose, squirrels, beavers, ducks, and turkeys. Some meat and fish were preserved for later use in the winter.

ASK QUESTIONS
As I read, I ask myself the following questions:
- ☐ How many people lived in a typical village?
- ☐ What did their homes look like?
- ☐ How did they make their canoes?
- ☐ What kinds of fish did they catch?

What other questions would you ask?

_____

_____

Women gathered berries, nuts and other wild plants. Children helped gather berries and wild rice. Women were also in charge of growing corn, squash, beans, potatoes and other vegetables. Corn was the major food in their diet. Women crushed corn in stone bowls to make the flour used in breads or stews.

THINK ABOUT WHAT IS IMPORTANT
This paragraph seems important. It tells what things the women and children did, and what kinds of foods they grew.

What other information do you think is important in this article?

_____

_____

UNLAWFUL TO PHOTOCOPY

GOING BEYOND THE READING

After reading a selection, a good reader thinks about what he or she has learned. Here, the reader learned interesting facts about the American Indian tribes once living around the Great Lakes.

After reading this article, the reader might:

★ add some new words — like *canoe*, *fibers* or *preserved* — to a list of vocabulary words;

★ search the Internet for more information about the Great Lakes tribes;

★ go to the library to take out books about other American Indian tribes from New York State;

★ plan a family trip to visit the area around the Great Lakes; or

★ visit an American Indian reservation located in New York State.

UNLAWFUL TO PHOTOCOPY

CHAPTER 2

READING LITERATURE

In the fourth grade, you will learn about reading two main types of texts — literary and informational. A **literary text** is written, not to tell you a set of facts, but to instruct and delight you. There are many types of literary texts, including stories, legends, poems, novels, and plays.

STORIES

We read stories for enjoyment. Good stories can help us imagine what it would be like to live in faraway places or to enjoy exciting adventures. They teach us about other people's experiences and lives. Stories put us in touch with all kinds of emotions. They can make us laugh, cry, or make our hearts pound with excitement.

THE ELEMENTS OF A STORY

Just as every house has a floor and a roof, every good story is made up of different elements that the story-writer must bring together. These elements of a story are known as:

setting   character   plot   theme

UNLAWFUL TO PHOTOCOPY

Read the following story about an emperor and his new clothes.

THE EMPEROR'S NEW CLOTHES

Several hundred years ago a wealthy emperor lived in Europe. He was quite fond of beautiful new clothes. He did not care about his soldiers or his people unless it was to show off his new clothes.

One day two thieves came to the town. The two thieves told everybody they were master tailors who could weave the most marvelous clothing. Not only were the colors and patterns of these clothes extraordinary, but the cloth had the strange quality of being invisible to anyone *unfit for his job* or *very stupid*.

"This is marvelous," the emperor thought when he heard of the master tailors. "If I had clothes cut from that material, I would know which of my counselors was unfit for his job. They must weave some material for me!" He gave the thieves a large sum of money to start working without delay.

The thieves set up a loom and acted as if they were weaving. The fine gold threads they demanded from the emperor were never used. Each night they sat before their empty looms, pretending to weave.

"I would like to know if my new clothes are finished. I will send my Prime Minister to see the weavers," thought the emperor. "He will know how to judge the material, for he is both clever and fit for his job."

The Prime Minister visited the weavers but saw only an empty loom. He thought, "I can't see a thing! Am I stupid? I can't believe it. Maybe I am not fit for my job. I had better not admit I can't see what they're weaving."

"Tell us what you think," demanded the thieves.

CONTINUED ▶

"It's beautiful. What patterns! What colors! I shall tell the emperor I'm greatly pleased," the Prime Minister answered. The two thieves now demanded even more money and greater quantities of gold thread. They said they needed it for weaving, but the loom remained as empty as ever.

Next, the emperor sent other ministers to see how the work was progressing. "Isn't it a marvelous piece of material?" asked the thieves as they described the beauty of the clothes to the ministers. "I'm not stupid," each minister repeated to himself, thinking he must be unfit for his job. Each one praised the loveliness of the clothing's patterns and colors.

At last the emperor decided to see the garment himself. With the most important people in his empire, he arrived where the weavers were hard at work at their loom.

"I can't see a thing!" thought the emperor. "This is a disaster! Am I stupid? Am I not fit to be emperor?" But aloud he said, "The clothes are very lovely. They have my approval."

The next day, the new clothes were ready for the emperor to wear in a parade. "Will Your Majesty please take off your clothes?" asked the thieves. "We shall help you put on your new clothes."

The thieves lifted their arms as if holding something in their hands and said, "These are the trousers and robe. They are as light as if they were made of spider webs! It will be as if Your Majesty had almost nothing on, but that is their special beauty." The emperor did as he was told. The thieves acted as if they were dressing him in the clothes they had made. The emperor stood in front of a mirror admiring the clothes he couldn't see.

CONTINUED ➤

UNLAWFUL TO PHOTOCOPY

The emperor left to walk in the parade. All the people of the town, who had lined the streets, shouted to the emperor that his new clothes were beautiful. "What a magnificent robe! How well the emperor's clothes fit!"

None of the people were willing to admit that they did not see a thing; for if anyone did, then he would be thought stupid or unfit for the job he held.

And then from the crowd, a little child cried out: "But the emperor doesn't have anything on!" "Listen to the little one," said the proud father. The people began to whisper to each other and repeated what the child had said.

"He doesn't have anything on! There's a child who says that the emperor has nothing on!" At last, the people began to shout, "He has nothing on!"

The emperor shivered, for he was certain that they were right; but he thought, "I must hold my head high and put up with it until the parade is over." And he walked even more proudly, while across town the two thieves made their escape.

BEING AN ACTIVE READER

★ Have you heard this story before?

★ How did you imagine the emperor looked in his new clothes?

★ Were you able to predict what happened in the story?

★ Does the story remind you of anything that happened in your own life?

Now, let's take a look at all four parts of a story — its *setting*, *character*, *plot*, and *theme*.

THE SETTING

The story setting is *when* and *where* the story takes place. A story may have more than one setting if events occur at different times and places. A story setting can take place in the past, present, or future, or even in an imaginary world where time hardly seems to exist. *The Emperor's New Clothes* takes place hundreds of years ago in a make-believe empire.

UNLAWFUL TO PHOTOCOPY

THE CHARACTERS

The characters are who the story is about. Characters can be made-up people or real people in a make-believe setting. Story characters may even be animals. Most stories have only one or two main characters. When reading a story, ask yourself the following questions about its characters:

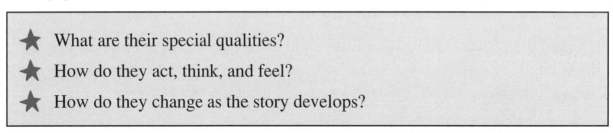

★ What are their special qualities?

★ How do they act, think, and feel?

★ How do they change as the story develops?

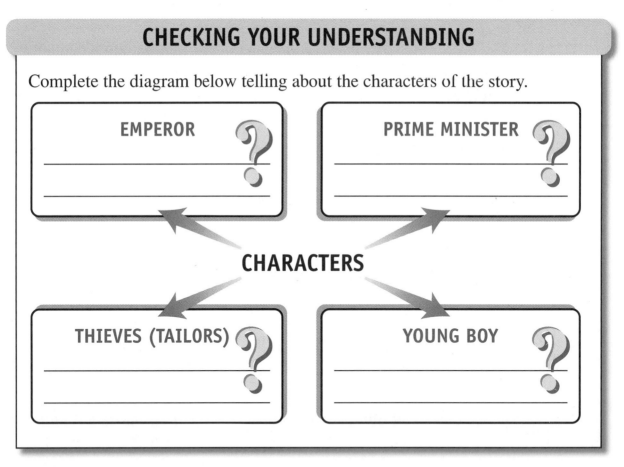

CHECKING YOUR UNDERSTANDING

Complete the diagram below telling about the characters of the story.

EMPEROR

PRIME MINISTER

CHARACTERS

THIEVES (TAILORS)

YOUNG BOY

THE PLOT

The plot is what happens in the story. It is made up of the events of the story. In almost all stories, characters face one or more problems. For example, a character may have a disagreement with another character in the story. As different events take place, the characters try to solve the main problem in the story.

UNLAWFUL TO PHOTOCOPY

When you read a story, ask yourself these questions about the plot:

 What **problems** do the main characters face?

 What **events** in the story affect these problems?

 What **actions** do the characters take to deal with these problems?

 How are these problems finally **resolved**?

CHECKING YOUR UNDERSTANDING

It often helps to make a diagram to follow the plot of a story. Complete the diagram below. In each box, put an important event from the story. Place these events in the order in which they occurred. The first two events have been completed for you:

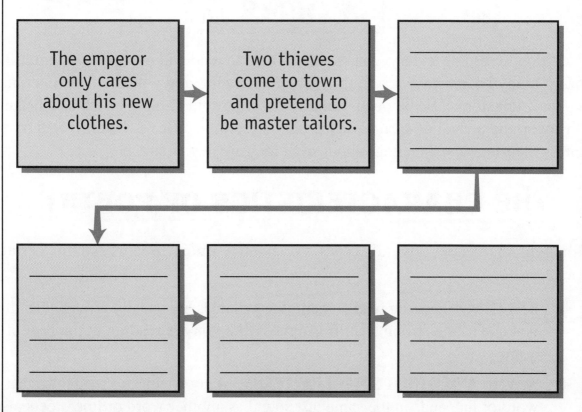

Another way to remember a story is by drawing pictures. Create a comic strip telling the main events of the story, *The Emperor's New Clothes*. Remember, it is *not* your art work that is important, but how well you show the story. Use a separate sheet of paper to create your comic strip.

UNLAWFUL TO PHOTOCOPY

THE STORY THEME OR LESSON

Stories often interest us because they teach us a message or lesson we can apply in our own lives. This message or lesson is called the **theme** of the story. A story may have one or more themes. The theme is why the story is important. For example, in *The Emperor's New Clothes*, one lesson is that we should not let others trick us into believing what we know is not true.

CHECKING YOUR UNDERSTANDING

Can you think of any other theme or lesson from this story? Briefly describe another **theme** of *The Emperor's New Clothes*.

_____

POEMS

In addition to reading a story, you should be able to read and interpret a **poem**. Like stories, many poems have a setting, characters, a plot, and a theme. However, not all poems tell stories. Some poems simply describe something — such as a beautiful flower, the arrival of spring, or the poet's feelings of love. Often, poets try to express their innermost feelings about what they are describing.

THE CHARACTERISTICS OF POETRY

Although there are several types of poetry, most poems share certain characteristics.

★ **RHYTHM.** When you read a poem, the syllables are usually arranged so that you can hear a strong beat. It is almost like you are reading to the beat of a drum.

★ **RHYME AND OTHER SOUND PATTERNS.** Many poems are written so that a word or line ends in the same last sound as another word or line. Poets also use other sound patterns to give poetry a musical quality. For example, they may use a series of words that begin with the same sound, like "soft as skin."

★ **IMAGERY.** Poets make use of appealing images or word pictures to express their feelings and ideas. Poets try to appeal to all our senses.

Unlawful to Photocopy

UNDERSTANDING POETRY

The first thing you should ask yourself when reading a poem is whether the poem tells a story or describes something. If the poet is telling a story, then you should try to keep track of all the story elements, just like any other story. For other poems, you should identify what the poet is describing and the poet's feelings about it.

Let's look at an actual poem. As you can see below, poetry is organized by lines instead of full sentences. When reading a poem, the reader usually pauses at the end of each line. Several lines of poetry are organized into something similar to paragraphs, known as **stanzas**. The poem *Whispers* has three stanzas. After reading the poem, analyze it by completing the box below.

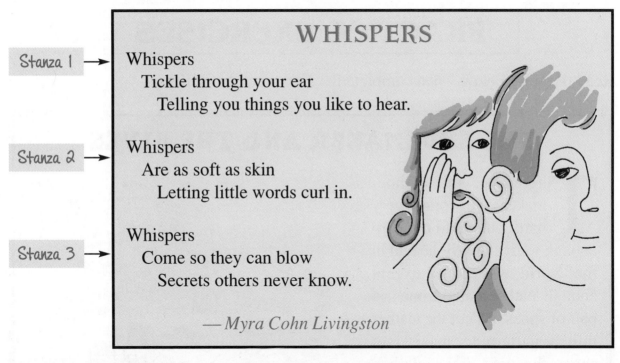

WHISPERS

Stanza 1 →
Whispers
    Tickle through your ear
        Telling you things you like to hear.

Stanza 2 →
Whispers
    Are as soft as skin
        Letting little words curl in.

Stanza 3 →
Whispers
    Come so they can blow
        Secrets others never know.

— *Myra Cohn Livingston*

ANALYZING A POEM

What is the poem about? _____

_____

What are the poet's feeling about this subject? _____

_____

Circle all the rhyming words in the poem.

UNLAWFUL TO PHOTOCOPY

In this case, the poet is not telling a story. She is describing whispers. She uses different sound devices and images in the poem to express her feelings. The word "whisper" itself sounds like the kind of soft sound that whispering makes. The word "soft" also sounds gentle and soft. The poet specially selects these words to help us imagine the sound of a whisper.

She also creates vivid images. To show that whispers are quiet and soft, she comparcs them to "soft skin." Her images appeal to all of our senses. In the first stanza, we feel the *tickle* of the whisper. In the second stanza, we *hear* its softness. We not only hear and feel the softness of a whisper — we also sense the close ties between the people who are whispering.

PRACTICE EXERCISES

Read the story below. Then complete the story map that follows.

THE SHOEMAKER AND THE ELVES

There once was a shoemaker who worked very hard, but could not earn enough to live on. All he had in the world was gone, except enough leather to make one last pair of shoes. He cut the leather into a pattern to make into shoes the next day and then went to bed.

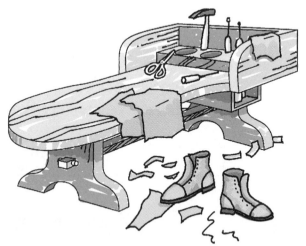

In the morning, when he sat down to work, the shoes were already made — and as beautiful as they could be. That day a customer came in and paid a high price for the shoes.

The poor shoemaker then bought enough leather to make two more pairs. That evening, he cut the patterns again and went to bed.

Unlawful to Photocopy

CONTINUED ⟶

When he got up the next morning, the shoes were again finished. Two buyers came in, and they, too, paid him well for the shoes. So he now bought leather for four pairs. Again, he cut the leather at night and found new shoes finished in the morning. This went on for some time, and the shoemaker became successful again.

One evening the shoemaker said to his wife, "I want to stay up and watch who comes and does my work for me." So he and his wife hid behind a curtain and watched to see what would happen.

At midnight, two little elves sat down at his bench and began to work, quickly stitching and tapping away. When the elves finished, they ran off, as quick as lightning.

The next day his wife said, "These elves have made us rich. We ought to do them a good deed in return. They must be cold, running about with hardly anything on. I will make each of them a shirt, a coat, a vest, and a pair of pants. You make each of them a little pair of shoes." The shoemaker agreed.

When all the things were ready, he and his wife laid them on the table. Then they went and hid behind the curtain.

At midnight, the elves came in to work as usual when they saw the clothes. They laughed in surprise as they dressed themselves in the twinkling of an eye. Then they danced around the room and out the door.

The shoemaker never saw them again, but everything went well with him from that time forward.

UNLAWFUL TO PHOTOCOPY

There are many ways to show information about a story. Below is one suggested way of summarizing a story. Complete the missing information.

STORY MAPPING

TITLE: _____

SETTING:

★ **Where:** _____

★ **When:** _____

MAIN CHARACTERS:

★ **Who:** _____

★ **Who:** _____

PLOT: *(List key events in the order that they happened)*

❶ _____

❷ _____

❸ _____

❹ _____

❺ _____

THEME OR LESSON:

★ _____

★ _____

UNLAWFUL TO PHOTOCOPY

Directions: Read the following poem. Then complete the exercise that follows:

SEA CALM

How still,
How strangely still
The water is today.
It is not good
For water,
To be so still that way.

— *Langston Hughes*

ANALYZING A POEM

1. What is this poem about? Use details from the poem to support your answer.

_____

_____

_____

2. What are the poet's feeling about this topic? Use details from the poem to support your answer.

_____

_____

_____

_____

Unlawful to Photocopy

CHAPTER 3

READING FOR INFORMATION

A second type of reading you should be able to recognize is an informational reading, sometimes called *nonfiction*. **Informational readings** are about real people, places, and events. The aim of an informational reading is to **inform** the reader.

There are many different types of informational texts. Some of the most common types you will learn about this school year are articles, editorials, and biographies:

★ **ARTICLES.** An article is a short informational piece. Articles are often found in newspapers, magazines, and encyclopedias. They tell about events, people, or any other subject.

★ **ESSAY.** An essay is a short writing expressing an author's views or opinions. Essays can be funny or serious, personal or persuasive.

★ **BIOGRAPHY.** A biography is an informational text that focuses on telling about the life and accomplishments of an individual person. A biography that someone writes about his or her own life, a *self*-biography, is called an **autobiography**.

All informational texts have some things in common. They all give the reader information about a **topic**. A topic is a subject. The topic of an informational text could be any subject — Chinese food, life in ancient Egypt, baseball, space travel or anything else you can think of. Usually, informational texts will tell the *who*, *what*, *when*, *where*, *why*, and *how* of a topic.

UNLAWFUL TO PHOTOCOPY

THE PARTS OF AN INFORMATIONAL READING

Just as stories have different parts, so do informational readings. There are *two* major parts to an informational reading:

The **main idea** says something about the general topic of the reading. The **supporting details** are facts and examples that explain, describe and illustrate the main idea.

To see how these parts work, let's first look at a short informational reading.

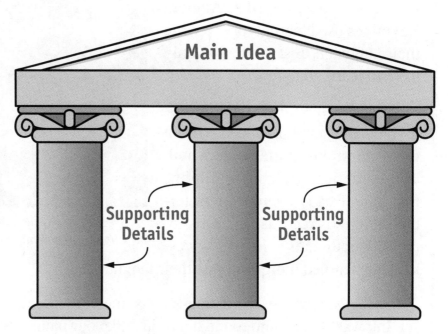

A Cobblestone Publication

February 1999	Vol. 7, Number 5

SCHOOL DAYS
by Joyce Haynes

In ancient Egypt, only the very smartest children went to school, where they learned to read and write. Most Egyptians never learned to read and write.

The children who went to school learned to be scribes. Scribes were very important people in ancient Egypt because they were almost the only ones who

UNLAWFUL TO PHOTOCOPY

CONTINUED

could read and write. Although records tell us that there were a few female scribes, most were men. Boys entered scribal school when they were quite young and studied hard for about 10 to 12 years.

It took years to learn how to write the hundreds of different symbols called **hieroglyphs**. Ancient Egyptians used hieroglyphs to write their language. Just think, you only have to learn 26 letters!

Students memorized the hieroglyphic signs and practiced writing them on stone, pottery, or wood. They practiced by copying things that had already been written: letters, religious records, and government documents. In this way, students learned more than just their language.

Hieroglyphics on the walls of the Temple of Amenophs III, around 1360 B.C.

Scribal students used writing tools somewhat like the parts of a water color set. Ink was shaped into round disks, just like our paint sets. But instead of many colors, scribes used only red and black. The cakes of ink were made out of a mineral called red ochre, and out of black carbon from burnt sticks or pans. Scribes carried small pots of water to mix with the inks. Their brushes, made of plants, were held in a small case.

Students often practiced writing on flat pieces of the limestone rock that could be found everywhere in Egypt. Many school texts, or homework, have been found on these flakes of stone. Sometimes a student or a scribe needed to write something very important. Then he wrote on papyrus paper, made from the reeds found along the Nile.

Tools used by Egyptian scribes — papyrus, ink palette, and a writing tool.

CONTINUED →

UNLAWFUL TO PHOTOCOPY

When a student finished scribe school, he could get a good job in ancient Egypt. He might become a doctor or a priest, the secretary to a noble family, the boss of a group of workers, or have some other job that required the ability to read and write.

The Egyptians wrote many different kinds of things, just as we do. They wrote letters home and sent bills for work they had done. They wrote poetry and stories and put down words of wisdom and advice for their children. They wrote many prayers to their gods.

You may want to look back at this article as you answer the following questions:

BEING AN ACTIVE READER

1. What did you already know about the topic of the article? _____

   _____

   _____

2. What did you learn that was new? _____

   _____

   _____

3. Imagine you are watching a scribe write a letter for someone. Describe what you see, using one or more of your senses.

   _____

   _____

THE MAIN IDEA OF A READING

UNLAWFUL TO PHOTOCOPY

The most important point that an author makes about the topic of a reading is known as its **main idea**. For example, an author may feel that a person is very kind. This could be the author's main idea. The author shows this by telling about the person's good deeds. Or the author may feel that a place is very dangerous. The author shows this by writing about the dangers to visitors.

Remember, the *main idea* is not any particular detail. It is what the reading is about *as a whole*. It is the most important idea in the reading. All the details in the reading should be connected to this main idea.

When you read a selection for information, there are several ways of finding the main idea.

LOOKING FOR A STATEMENT OF THE MAIN IDEA

One way to find the main idea of a reading is to look at the title to see if it is a direct statement of the main idea. Sometimes the author tells you what the main idea is in a special sentence at the beginning or end of the passage. First, examine the title to see if it states the main idea. Then, look at the first few paragraphs and the conclusion to see if one of the topic sentences states the main idea.

THE TOPIC APPROACH

A second way to find the main idea of a reading is to use the "topic approach." Think of this approach as a giant funnel — having a large opening at the top and a smaller opening at the bottom. This "funnel" can help lead you to the main idea.

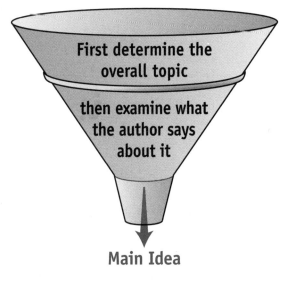

First determine the overall topic

then examine what the author says about it

Main Idea

* **First**, decide on the overall topic of the selection. Remember that the topic is the subject of the reading.

* **Then**, carefully examine what the author says about the topic.

Let's look at each of these steps more closely.

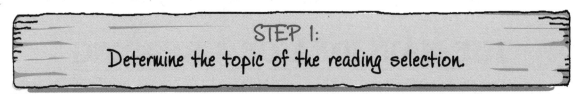

STEP 1:
Determine the topic of the reading selection.

UNLAWFUL TO PHOTOCOPY

Begin by determining the general **subject** or **topic** of the selection. Is it about a person, place, or event? Think of the topic as the opening of a funnel. It should be large enough to take in everything discussed in the reading. Often, the title identifies the topic. The topic of the article on pages 23 through 25 was the education of scribes of ancient Egypt. Everything in the article relates to those scribes.

STEP 2:
See what the writer is saying overall about the topic.

Once you have decided on the topic, focus on what the writer has to say about it. You can use the "topic approach" even when the main idea is not directly stated by the author. Look for the author's overall **message** about the topic. This message is the author's main idea. Other details in the reading should explain or support this main idea. They will often tell about the *who*, *what*, *when*, *where*, *why*, and *how*. The main idea is what connects these details together.

In the reading passage about Egyptian scribes, the author's main idea seems to be that it was difficult but rewarding to become a scribe in ancient Egypt. Many facts mentioned throughout the article help to support this main idea.

RELATING IDEAS AND DETAILS

A third way to find the main idea is to use the "ideas and details" approach. For this approach, simply list all the major ideas and details in the selection. You can either write these out or list them in your mind. Then look over what you have listed. See if one idea covers or connects all the others. The **main idea** will be the *single most important idea* in the story or article. For example, let's try this approach with the article "School Days." In this article, if you were to list the important ideas and major details, your list might look like this:

IMPORTANT IDEAS AND DETAILS

★ Only the smartest children went to school and learned to read and write.

★ Boys entered school and studied for 10 to 12 years to become scribes.

★ There were hundreds of hieroglyphs to learn in ancient Egypt.

★ Scribes could get good jobs in ancient Egypt.

★ In ancient Egypt, scribes wrote for many purposes.

★ Scribes had great importance, but becoming a scribe was difficult.

UNLAWFUL TO PHOTOCOPY

Which of these important ideas and major details is general enough to connect all of the other items? The answer to this question will be the **main idea** of the passage. Sometimes the main idea connecting these details is not stated directly. Then you have to think of a main idea yourself that connects all the others.

When asked about the main idea, use either the:

direct statement approach   **topic approach**   **ideas-and-details approach**

Practice using each of these approaches to see which one works best for you. Start thinking about the main idea as soon as you begin reading an informational passage. You can change what you think the main idea is as you read more. Often the author will just tell readers the main idea of the passage. Be sure to look at the title, subheadings, illustration captions and conclusion for clues to the main idea.

THE SUPPORTING DETAILS

To help the reader understand the main idea, an author supplies **examples**, **details**, and **illustrations**. Each of these helps to support the author's main idea. It is through the use of these details and examples that the author explains the main idea or tries to prove that it is correct.

CHECKING YOUR UNDERSTANDING

Look at some of the details listed in the chart on page 27. Which of these details support the idea that scribes were both important in ancient Egypt and faced hard work? Explain your answer.

_____

_____

_____

UNLAWFUL TO PHOTOCOPY

Use the illustration below to check your answers from the previous page.

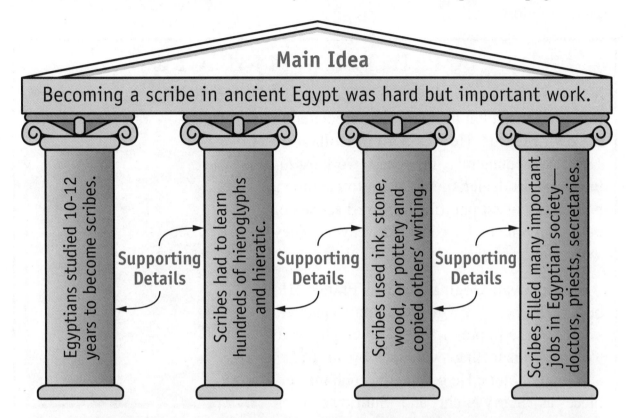

Main Idea

Becoming a scribe in ancient Egypt was hard but important work.

Egyptians studied 10-12 years to become scribes.

Supporting Details

Scribes had to learn hundreds of hieroglyphs and hieratic.

Supporting Details

Scribes used ink, stone, wood, or pottery and copied others' writing.

Supporting Details

Scribes filled many important jobs in Egyptian society—doctors, priests, secretaries.

SUMMARY

In Chapters 2 and 3, you learned about two different types of readings.

IN A STORY

In a story, you can expect to find a <u>setting</u>, <u>characters</u>, <u>plot</u>, and <u>theme</u>.

IN AN INFORMATIONAL READING

In an informational reading, you can expect to find a topic, a main idea about that topic, and <u>supporting details</u>. Supporting details may include descriptions, facts, and examples.

UNLAWFUL TO PHOTOCOPY

Directions: Use the information in the passage about Beijing to complete the graphic organizer below.

A PAINTER'S STRUGGLE

Vincent Van Gogh is now one of the world's favorite artists, but he was not appreciated in his own lifetime. He was born in Holland in 1853. As a young man, he went to work for his uncle, an art dealer, and decided to become a painter. His first paintings showed scenes of poor coal miners, farmers, and weavers. They were painted in dark and gloomy colors.

Later, Van Gogh moved to France. He became friends with a group of French painters known as the Impressionists. Van Gogh began to express his feelings with thick brush strokes and lively colors. He completed such master-pieces as "Starry Night,"and "Sunflowers."

Sunflowers by Vincent van Gogh

Van Gogh suffered from fits of loneliness and despair. He exhibited only a few of his paintings. These were not well received by the public. In 1890, Van Gogh took his own life. He was 37 years old.

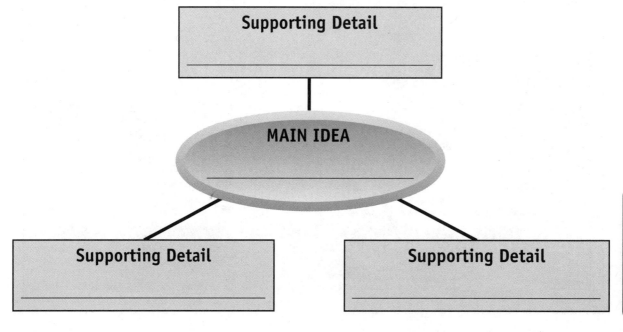

Supporting Detail

_____

MAIN IDEA

_____

Supporting Detail

_____

Supporting Detail

_____

Unlawful to Photocopy

SESSION 1: READING

Session 1 of the **New York's Grade 4 English Language Arts Test** consists of several reading passages. Each passage is followed by a series of multiple-choice questions. Each question has four possible choices. Your task is to select the best of the four choices to answer the question.

The multiple-choice questions on **Session 1** of the test can be grouped into three main types. These multiple-choice questions test your ability to:

understand what the whole reading is about

understand specific information in the reading

apply information from the reading or make conclusions from the reading

The next five chapters will examine these different types of questions in more detail. Chapter 9 has a practice test just like **Session 1** of the actual English Language Arts Test you will take later this school year.

Unlawful to Photocopy

CHAPTER 4

WORD-MEANING QUESTIONS

Some of the questions on the **Grade 4 English Language Arts Test** will check how well you understand the meaning of a word or group of words in a reading passage.

DEFINING A WORD

Most *word-meaning questions* will simply ask you what a word or phrase means. For example, read the paragraph below. It introduces the story of **King Midas** as retold by Nathaniel Hawthorne, a famous American writer. Midas was given the unique power to turn everything he touched into gold. Some of the more difficult words in the passage are bolded.

King Midas was *fonder* of gold than anything else in the world. He *valued* his royal crown chiefly because it was *composed* of that precious metal. If he loved anything better or half so well, it was the one little maiden who played so *merrily* around her father's *footstool*. But the more Midas loved his daughter, the more did he desire and seek wealth. He thought, foolish man, that the best thing he could possibly do for his dear child would be to *bequeath* her the immensest pile of yellow *glistening* coin that ever had been heaped together since the world was made. Thus, he gave all his thoughts and all his time to this purpose.

Now that you have finished reading this paragraph, let's see how well you can answer some *word-meaning questions* based on this passage.

Unlawful to Photocopy

1 In this paragraph, the word *composed* means

A peaceful

B made up

C tired

D ground up

EXPLAINING YOUR ANSWER

What is the answer? _____ Explain why you picked that answer.

_____

_____

How would you answer this question if you were unsure about the meaning of *composed*? There are four methods you can use to figure out the meaning of this or any other word (or group of words):

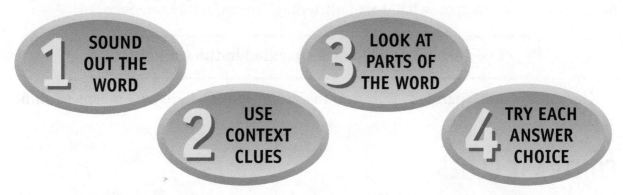

1 SOUND OUT THE WORD

2 USE CONTEXT CLUES

3 LOOK AT PARTS OF THE WORD

4 TRY EACH ANSWER CHOICE

Not every method will always work. However, you can often combine several of these methods to help you figure out the meaning of an unknown word.

SOUND OUT THE WORD

To sound out a word, say the sounds of the syllables that make up the word. By sounding out a word, you may find it is a word you know or like one you know.

Let's try to sound out the word "compose." First break down the word into syllables (*its smaller parts*): **com-pose.** Then use the sounds of the letters to say each syllable. Does this sound like any word that you already know? For example, have you ever used the word *compos*ition? If it does, check the answer choices to see if you can find the correct answer.

UNLAWFUL TO PHOTOCOPY

USE CONTEXT CLUES

Surrounding words and sentences often provide clues to the meaning of a difficult word or phrase. These are called **context clues**. On the test, there will often be some context clues to help you answer any *word-meaning question*. In fact, there are several types of context clues you can use to figure out the meaning of an unfamiliar word or phrase.

DEFINING CLUES

Sometimes context clues provide words with similar meanings or even define the difficult word. For example, what does "glistening" mean in this sentence?

> **The glistening gold coins sparkled in the sunlight.**

Here, the word "sparkled" tells you the definition. To "glisten" means to shine or sparkle.

CONTRAST CLUES

Sometimes context clues will tell you what a word is **not**. For example:

> **Unlike his sad wife, King Midas felt rather jovial.**

In this example, the sentence provides an important clue to the meaning of *jovial*. The sentence tells you that Midas is not feeling like his wife. His wife is sad, but he is *jovial*. From this contrast, you should be able to figure out that the word *jovial* means the opposite of sad, or someone who is happy.

COMMON-SENSE CLUES

Sometimes you need to look through an entire paragraph to find context clues. A series of details may hint at what a word or phrase means. You then have to apply your own common sense to figure this meaning out. The following page describes some of the most frequent common-sense clues:

UNLAWFUL TO PHOTOCOPY

★ **Part of a Series.** If the word is part of a series of things, it often names something similar to other items in the series. For example:

> *King Midas feared falling over the dangerous, sharp, **precipitous** cliff.*

In this example, *precipitous* is part of a series of words describing the cliff. You might guess that it has something in common with *sharp* and *dangerous*. This could lead you to understand that *precipitous* means very steep.

★ **Examples.** A reading passage may give examples of what a word or phrase is supposed to identify. Knowing one or more examples of the word can help you to figure out what it means. For example:

> *King Midas became a **philanthropist** who gave gold to*
> *build temples and to feed the poor.*

What do you think a *philanthropist* means in this sentence? The examples indicate that someone who is a *philanthropist* gives money to help people.

★ *Cause and Effect.* The passage may describe a cause or effect of the unfamiliar word. Such clues can often help you figure out what the word means:

> He valued his royal crown chiefly because
> it was ***composed*** of that precious metal.

In this sentence, Midas thinks his crown is valuable *because* it is *composed* of gold. Being *composed* of gold has the effect of making the crown valuable and expensive. From this clue, what do you think *composed* means?

★ *Describing a Situation.* An unfamiliar word or phrase may identify a situation described in the text. In this case, look at the description carefully to figure out what the word means. For example:

> But the more Midas loved his daughter, the more did he desire and seek wealth. He thought, foolish man, that the best thing he could possibly do for his dear child would be to ***bequeath*** her the immensest pile of yellow, glistening coin that ever had been heaped together since the world was made.

UNLAWFUL TO PHOTOCOPY

By carefully examining the surrounding sentences, you can get some sense of what *bequeath* might mean. Midas loves his daughter. He also desires and seeks wealth. He thinks the best thing he can do for his daughter is to bequeath her wealth — a huge pile of yellow, glistening coins. From these surrounding sentences, you can get the idea that to *bequeath* is to leave someone a valuable gift when a person dies.

★ **The Mood of the Passage.** The *style*, *mood*, and *tone* of the selection can also help you figure out what an unfamiliar word or phrase might mean.

- Is the author writing about something happy or sad?

- Is the selection funny or serious?

Often the correct answer choice will be the one that best fits with the mood of the selection or the author's viewpoint. For example, the tone of the paragraph on page 32 is serious but cheerful. In answering *word-meaning questions* about this paragraph, you should **avoid** any choices that appear to be overly sad or tragic. These would probably not be correct, since they would not be in keeping with the general message and tone.

PARTS-OF-SPEECH CLUES

Another type of clue is the *part of speech* of the unfamiliar word. Look at how the unfamiliar word is used in the sentence. Does it tell about an action (*verb*), name a thing (*noun*), or describe something (*adjective*)? The correct answer should play the same role in the sentence as the unknown word. For example:

King Midas was ***fonder*** of gold than of anything else in the world.

Notice how the word *fonder* is used in the sentence to describe how Midas felt about gold. The sentence tells us that Midas was *fonder* of gold than anything else in the world. The correct answer must also be an adjective describing how someone feels.

LOOK AT PARTS OF THE WORD

Many words are made up of different parts. For example, *footstool* brings together the words **foot** and **stool**. It is a special stool for resting one's feet.

UNLAWFUL TO PHOTOCOPY

Prefixes. Some words have special beginnings, called **prefixes**. Knowing certain common *prefixes* can help you figure out the meaning of an unknown word. For example, *re*view, *re*read and *re*turn all begin with the prefix *re*. Usually *re* in front of a word means "to do again."

Other common prefixes turn a word into its opposite — for example, *un*, *in*, and *dis* all mean **not**. You can see this in the following words: *usual* becomes *unusual*; *sincere* changes to *insincere*; and *similar* turns to *dissimilar*. Sometimes a prefix has more than one meaning. The prefix *in* can also mean *inside* — such as *indoors*.

Suffixes. Special endings, known as **suffixes**, also help provide clues about the meaning of an unknown word. For example, *painful* means something that is *full* of pain. *Careful* describes a person who is *full* of care. In those examples, *ful* is the suffix.

Separating a word from its suffix often helps you to understand its meaning. Many common suffixes change the part of speech of a word — *ly*, *er*, *ion*, *al*, *ness*, and *ment*.

quick	quick**ly**	govern	govern**ment**
associate	associat**ion**	happy	happi**ness**
continue	continu**al**	teach	teach**er**

Sometimes it helps to cover the front or back of a difficult word to see if you recognize the word without its beginning or ending (*known as the root*). For example, let's look at the word **merrily** from the sample paragraph on page 32. Do any of this word's parts remind you of other words you know? If you cover the end of the word, you can see part of the word **merry**. **Merry** means happy. Looking at the different parts of a word, when used together with context clues, can often help you to figure out its meaning.

TRY EACH ANSWER CHOICE

The last method for answering a *word-meaning question* is to substitute each answer choice in place of the unfamiliar word. Think about what the author is trying to say in the sentence. Select the word or group of words that seems to make the most sense.

UNLAWFUL TO PHOTOCOPY

For example, look back at the question and answer choices earlier on page 33. Read each one in place of *composed* in the sentence:

"He valued his royal crown chiefly because it was composed of that precious metal."

> **A** He valued his royal crown chiefly because it was [*peaceful*] of that precious metal.
>
> **B** He valued his royal crown chiefly because it was [*made up*] of that precious metal.
>
> **C** He valued his royal crown chiefly because it was [*tired*] of that precious metal.
>
> **D** He valued his royal crown chiefly because it was [*ground up*] of that precious metal.

★ **Choice A** must be wrong. Midas does not value his crown because it is peaceful.

★ **Choice C** is wrong. The crown is not tired, which makes no sense at all.

★ **Choice D** is also wrong. Midas' crown is not being ground up, which also makes no sense.

You can see that the best answer is choice **B**. It is the correct answer because when "made up" is placed in the sentence, it is logical and reasonable. Midas values his crown because it is made up of gold. *Composed* must therefore mean to be "made up" of something.

SIMILAR AND OPPOSITE WORDS

On the **Grade 4 English Language Arts Test**, you might be asked to select a word with the *same* or *opposite meaning* of a word used in the passage. First, you must try to find what the word in the passage means. Once you know this, examine the choices to select the word that is *most like* or *most unlike* the way the word is used in the passage.

UNLAWFUL TO PHOTOCOPY

Let's look at a sample question of this type.

2 Read this sentence.

The glistening gold coins sparkled in the sunlight.

Which word means the opposite of "glistening?"

A shiny   **C** quiet

B dull   **D** flavorful

EXPLAINING YOUR ANSWER

What is the answer? _____ Explain why you picked that answer.

_____

First, you must determine that *glistening* means something that is sparkling or shiny. You can eliminate **choice A**, which means the same as *glistening*. Carefully examine the choices that remain. You need a word that means the ***opposite of glistening***. What choice would you pick as the **opposite of shiny**?

SUMMARY: DEFINING A WORD

When you come across an unknown word in a reading selection, try using these methods to figure out the meaning of the word:

★ <u>Sound out the Word</u>. After you say it, see if you recognize the word.

★ <u>Use Context Clues</u>. Look for defining, contrasting, and common sense context clues.

★ <u>Use Parts of Speech Clues</u>. See how the unknown word is used in the sentence.

★ <u>Look at Parts of the Word</u>. See if you recognize the beginning or ending of the word, or the root word without its beginning or ending.

★ <u>Try Each Answer Choice</u>. Substitute each answer choice in place of the word. Select the answer that makes the most sense when substituted.

UNLAWFUL TO PHOTOCOPY

PRACTICE EXERCISE

THE PENNSYLVANIA DUTCH

The "Pennsylvania Dutch" do not come from Holland as their name might suggest. Instead, the Pennsylvania Dutch are the <u>descendants</u> of German immigrants in Pennsylvania who have kept their German language, heritage, and customs. Many of them follow the Amish religion — a form of Protestant Christianity.

Lancaster County, Pennsylvania, is the heart of Pennsylvania Dutch country. Small farms cover the hillsides. Thriving vegetable gardens <u>flourish</u> behind the farmhouses. The county <u>resembles</u> almost any farming region in America, but on closer inspection, no electric or telephone wires connect houses to lines along the road.

Today the Amish of Lancaster look and live much as they did two hundred years ago. Women's clothes lack zippers and buttons. The Amish consider these too fancy. There is no electrical power for farm work. Horses pull plows across the fields and black buggies into town. Farmhouses sometimes look <u>vacant</u> without curtains or lights in the windows.

1 In the first paragraph, the word "descendants" means

A partners in the same business
B children and later generations
C people having the same religion
D people who have lost their wealth

UNLAWFUL TO PHOTOCOPY

UNLOCKING THE ANSWER

🔑 **Sound out the word.** [de-scend-ant]
Do you recognize this word?

🔑 **Use context clues.**
★ They are descendants of German immigrants.
★ They have kept their German language, heritage and customs.

🔑 **Look at parts of the word.** descend-ant
Do any of these parts remind you of any word?
★ **Descend** means to *come down.*

🔑 **Try each answer choice.**
Read the answer choices in place of <u>descendant</u> in the sentence in the first paragraph.
★ *Which fits best as the answer?*

2 Read this sentence from the passage.

Thriving vegetable gardens flourish behind the farmhouses.

Which word means the same as "flourish"?

A thrive
B farm
C cover
D resemble

EXPLAINING YOUR ANSWER

What is the answer? _____ Explain why you picked that answer.

_____

_____

UNLAWFUL TO PHOTOCOPY

UNLOCKING THE ANSWER

This question asks you to choose the word most similar to *fluorish*.

🔑 **Use context clues.** From the paragraph, you can learn that "thriving vegetable gardens flourish." From these context clues in the sentence you can conclude that *flourish* probably has something to do with growing or doing well.

🔑 Based on these clues, what word do you think is most similar to *flourish*?

3 Read this sentence from the passage.

Farmhouses sometimes look vacant without curtains or lights in the window.

Which word means the opposite of "vacant?"

A empty

B pretty

C unfilled

D occupied

UNLOCKING THE ANSWER

🔑 To answer to this type of question, first determine the meaning of *vacant*. From context clues in the sentence you can conclude that *vacant* probably has something to do with empty or unoccupied, since "vacant" houses have no curtains or lights in the windows.

🔑 Based on these clues, what word do you think is the best choice for the opposite of *vacant*?

UNLAWFUL TO PHOTOCOPY

CHAPTER 5

FINDING THE MAIN IDEA

Some questions on the **Grade 4 English Language Arts Test** will check how well you understand the main idea of a reading. These questions may be stated in a variety of ways:

> **What is this article mainly about?**

> **What is the main idea of the reading passage?**

> **What would be the best title for the reading passage?**

This chapter will help you answer these types of questions. How you answer these *main idea questions* will depend on whether the reading selection is a *story*, *poem* or an *informational reading*. Let's examine each of these types to see how to find the main idea.

STORIES

When you see a question asking for the "main idea" of a story or what it is "mainly about," look for an answer choice that identifies the *problem* facing the main characters and shows how it is *solved*. The best answer will describe what happens in the *entire story*, rather than just a part of it.

Think of the "main idea" as a very short summary telling what is really important to the story. Less important details are left out. Just pretend your friend has asked you about a story you just finished reading. You have only **one sentence** to tell your friend about the story.

Sometimes a *main idea question* about a story asks for its theme or general lesson. Look carefully at the answer choices to see what the question is really asking for.

UNLAWFUL TO PHOTOCOPY

You will now read an Aesop's fable and get some practice in answering a question about the main idea.

THE HARE AND THE TORTOISE

A hare was making fun of a tortoise one day for being so slow. "Do you ever get anywhere?" the hare asked with a mocking laugh. "Yes," replied the tortoise, "and I get there sooner than you think. In fact, I'll run you a race and prove it."

The hare was very amused at the thought of running a race with the tortoise, and just for fun he agreed to do it. So the fox, who agreed to act as judge, marked the distance for the race and started the runners off.

The hare was soon far out of sight. To let the tortoise know how silly it was for him to challenge a speedy hare, the hare decided to lie down beside a tree to take a nap until the tortoise could catch up.

Meanwhile, the tortoise kept going slowly but steadily. After a time, the tortoise passed the place where the hare was sleeping. The hare slept on very peacefully. When at last he did wake up, the tortoise was already very near the finishing line. The hare now ran his swiftest, but could not overtake the tortoise in time.

1 The story "The Hare and the Tortoise" is mostly about how

    A a tortoise and hare decide to have a race

    B a tortoise beat an overconfident hare who slept during a race

    C a hare made fun of a slow-moving tortoise

    D a tortoise was so slow that other animals became upset

EXPLAINING YOUR ANSWER

What is the answer? _____ Explain why you picked that answer.

_____

UNLAWFUL TO PHOTOCOPY

Did you select the right answer? Three of the answer choices focus on details in the story rather than the story as a whole.

★ **Choice A** tells why the race was run, but it does not say who won the race or why.

★ **Choice C** tells how the hare made fun of the tortoise, but it does not say anything about the race.

★ **Choice D** tells about the tortoise, but it fails to say anything about the race.

Only **choice B** tells about the race, who won it, and why. It really gives the "main idea" of the fable — a slow tortoise races a speedy hare and is able to win the race because the hare is so overconfident he takes a nap in the middle of the race! Choice B is actually a one-sentence summary of the main events of the story. These are the really important things a person needs to know, to understand what the story is about.

When you see a *main idea* or *mostly about question* about a story, take the following steps:

UNLOCKING THE ANSWER

🔑 **First**, identify the main character or characters in the story.
★ What is the main problem they face?
★ How do they solve this problem?

🔑 **Next**, see if you can think of a *single sentence* that summarizes what happens in the story. Imagine you are telling a friend what the story is about. Make believe that you can use *one sentence* to tell your friend the main problem and how it was solved.

🔑 **Finally**, look at the answer choices. Pick the one choice that is closest to your sentence that tells the main idea of the entire story. Answers that give specific details from the story rather than the main idea will *not* be correct. If you are unsure of the correct answer, quickly reread the passage.

UNLAWFUL TO PHOTOCOPY

POEMS

You may also be asked to select the "main idea" of a poem. Remember that there are two types of poems. Some poems tell a story. Other poems express the poet's feelings about something — an event, an object, or another person.

★ If the poem tells a story, you should answer a *main idea question* about it the same way as you would answer any other *main idea question* about a story.

★ If the poem mainly expresses the poet's feelings about something, then the "main idea" should identify what the poet is writing about and how the poet feels about it.

THE LIBRARY
by Barbara A. Huff

It looks like any building
When you pass it on the street,
Made of stone and glass and marble,
Made of iron and concrete.

But once inside you can ride
A camel or a train,
Visit Rome, Siam, or Nome,
Feel a hurricane,
Meet a king, learn to sing,
How to bake a pie,
Go to sea, plant a tree,
Find how airplanes fly,
Train a horse, and of course
Have all the dogs you'd like,
See the moon, a sandy dune,
Or catch a whooping pike.

Everything that books can bring
You'll find inside those walls.
A world is there for you to share
When adventure calls.

You cannot tell its magic
By the way the building looks,
But there's wonderment within it,
The wonderment of books.

UNLAWFUL TO PHOTOCOPY

2 What is the main idea of the poem *The Library*?

    A Libraries are places that look like any other building.

    B Most libraries are made of stone, glass, marble and concrete.

    C Libraries allow people to imagine many experiences.

    D You cannot tell much about a library by the way it looks.

EXPLAINING YOUR ANSWER

What is the answer? _____ Explain why you picked that answer.

_____

_____

INFORMATIONAL READINGS

You already know that most informational readings have a main idea and supporting details. A *main idea question* about an informational reading will ask for the main idea in one of several ways:

| What is the passage mainly about? | What is the main idea of the passage? | What is the best title for the passage? |

Depending on the answer choices, you are being asked for either the **topic** of the passage or for a short statement of the author's **main idea**.

Remember, there are several ways to identify the **main idea** of an informational reading:

★ You can look for a direct statement of the main idea by the author. Often a sentence near the beginning or at the end of the reading states what the reading is mainly about.

★ You can determine the topic or subject of the reading. Then see what the author has to say about it.

★ You can list all the important ideas and facts mentioned in the reading. Then see which idea seems to connect to all the others.

Let's see how well you can identify the main idea of an informational passage. Read the article about cacao beans on the next page.

UNLAWFUL TO PHOTOCOPY

Cricket

Vol. 28, Number 12   **August, 2001**

WHEN MONEY GREW ON TREES
by Amy Butler Greenfield

Several thousand years ago, forest dwellers in Central America discovered an amazing tree in the rain forest. Small white flowers sprang from its branches and its trunk. The flowers ripened into red-and-yellow fruit. This fruit contained seeds, or beans, that humans could eat. The small brown beans were bitter, but had a flavor the forest dwellers liked.

By 500 B.C., people in Mexico and Central America were growing these cacao trees. Over time cacao beans became valuable — so valuable that Aztec rulers collected them as a tax. By the later 1400s, people were treating these beans like coins to buy food and clothing.

Cacao beans had other good points. They were cheap enough to be used for small purchases and usually lasted for several years. And, unlike coins, cacao beans could be eaten.

People with extra cacao beans drank *cacahuatl* (ka-ka-hwa-tel), a mixture of ground-up cacao beans, cold water, corn, and chili peppers. Some people liked to add vanilla and flowers to the mixture. Often they dyed the drink red. But no matter what color it was, *cacahuatl* was very spicy — and bitter! It didn't taste like the chocolate that we know today.

Europeans first saw cacao beans in 1502, when Christopher Columbus and his son stumbled across them. Neither of them understood how valuable the beans were. In 1519, however, when Cortés invaded Mexico, he discovered warehouses filled with cacao beans in the royal stronghold. Soon the Spaniards realized that cacao beans were like money in the Americas — money that grew on trees!

UNLAWFUL TO PHOTOCOPY

CONTINUED

Dreaming of riches, the Spaniards forced the native people to grow more and more cacao beans. Cacao beans poured into the conquerors' storehouses, even as the native people — and their land — suffered greatly.

To the Spaniards, cacao beans were money, not food. They refused to drink *cacahuatl*. They thought it looked like dirty water. When it was dyed red, some Spaniards felt it looked like blood.

In time, however, the Spaniards created their own version of the drink. They called it chocolate. Like the Aztec *cacahuatl*, Spanish chocolate was made with cacao beans, chili peppers, vanilla, and water. But unlike *cacahuatl*, chocolate did not have corn. Instead, it had sugar.

By the 1580s, the new beverage was very popular. People in the Spanish colonies sent cacao beans to friends in Spain so they could make chocolate, too. Their friends enjoyed the beverage, but made a few changes to it. Although some people in Spain continued to make chocolate with cold water, others preferred it hot. Many Spaniards added extra sugar to the recipe. Others added cinnamon and cloves.

Word of the drink spread to the rest of Europe. Over the next decades, Europeans added almonds, egg yolks, lemon peel, nutmeg, and melon seeds to their chocolate. They also added an ingredient familiar to us today: milk. To these people, cacao beans were food, not money. They never tried to use the beans as coins, and eventually the people of Spanish America stopped using them as currency, too.

3 Which sentence best summarizes the main idea of this article?

A The use of cacao beans changed from money to an ingredient in a drink.
B Aztecs used cacao beans as a form of money.
C Aztecs used cacao beans to make a spicy drink that was dyed red.
D The Spanish added sugar to crushed cacao beans.

Before you answer this question, let's see if we can point you in the right direction. The questions on the next page will help you find the correct answer.

UNLAWFUL TO PHOTOCOPY

POINTING THE WAY

➡ What is the **topic** of the reading? _____

➡ What is the author's **main idea** about this topic? _____

_____

_____

_____

_____

➡ Which answer choice is most like your main idea above? _____

Remember that some "mostly about" questions may ask you just for the **topic** of the reading. Look over the answer choices to see what kind of question it is. Then use the steps outlined below:

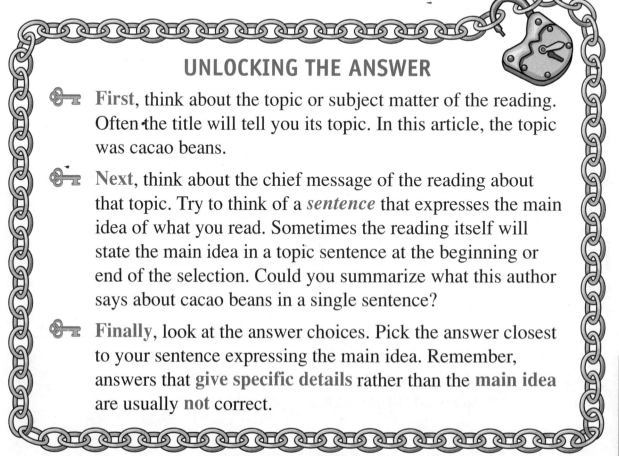

UNLOCKING THE ANSWER

First, think about the topic or subject matter of the reading. Often the title will tell you its topic. In this article, the topic was cacao beans.

Next, think about the chief message of the reading about that topic. Try to think of a *sentence* that expresses the main idea of what you read. Sometimes the reading itself will state the main idea in a topic sentence at the beginning or end of the selection. Could you summarize what this author says about cacao beans in a single sentence?

Finally, look at the answer choices. Pick the answer closest to your sentence expressing the main idea. Remember, answers that **give specific details** rather than the **main idea** are usually **not** correct.

UNLAWFUL TO PHOTOCOPY

PRACTICE EXERCISE

Let's put what you have learned to the test. Read the following passages and answer the questions that follow it. These questions are based on both this chapter and the previous chapter on *word-meaning questions*.

Invention Number Three
by Jeanne DiPrau

Ferguson Jones was planning to be a famous inventor. He was not famous yet, being only in the fourth grade, but he was on his way. Ferguson had just completed his first invention.

"Mom," Ferguson said. "My invention is ready. Step into my room. You too, Willard," he said to his brother, who was busy fixing the kitchen clock in their apartment. On the table in his bedroom was a contraption made of wooden sticks, cardboard tubes, and rubber bands. A red balloon was tied to the top.

"What's that?" said Willard.

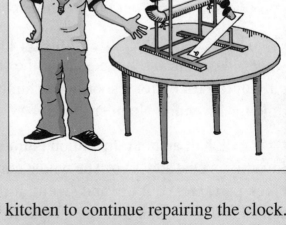

"Just watch," Ferguson said. "This invention works with chutes and levers." He unhooked a rubber band, which caused a chute to tip, which sent a ball rolling. The ball fell onto a lever with a tack at the end. The tack leaped up and pierced the balloon, which popped.

Ferguson's mother laughed. "Very clever!" she said.

"But not very useful," said Willard. "If you want to pop a balloon, just stick a pin in it!" Willard then returned to the kitchen to continue repairing the clock. He had the larger clock parts spread out on the table and the smaller parts lined up on the sill of the apartment house window.

Ferguson was sorry his brother didn't appreciate his invention. He knew all famous inventors were scoffed at early in their careers. He got right to work on Invention Number Two.

UNLAWFUL TO PHOTOCOPY

CONTINUED ▶

When he finished, he called in his mother and brother again. "I present Invention Number Two, which works with strings and wheels," said Ferguson. It was a network of strings that ran across Ferguson's room. "Watch this," Ferguson said, sitting on his bed. He turned a crank, which pulled a string, which caused other strings to move in a complicated way. On the other side of the room, one of Ferguson's tennis shoes, hooked to the end of the string, rose in the air and traveled toward his bed. Grinning, Ferguson reached up and grabbed his sneaker.

His mother chuckled. "That's ingenious!" she said. Willard then asked, "Why not invent something useful?"

Ferguson tried to think of a useful invention. But soon he realized that what he liked best was the invention itself — not what it could do. He liked figuring out what would happen if you pulled on this and pushed on that, if you put a weight here and used a balance there. What the invention actually *did* wasn't as interesting.

Just then Ferguson heard Willard yell from the kitchen. He dashed in to see Willard and Mom standing by the open window. "I just brushed it with my elbow and a part of the clock fell," Willard was saying.

"It's way down there on the fire escape steps," Willard said. He offered to climb down and get it, but Mom objected. She said, "It's too dangerous."

Ferguson peered out the apartment window. "Where is it?" he asked.

"There," said Willard, pointing. Ferguson looked, then saw it — a little wheel-like thing — on the edge of the step. He did some quick thinking. Tricky, but not too tricky for a soon-to-be famous inventor. "OK," said Ferguson. "It's time for Invention Number Three."

It took half an hour. Invention Number Three combined the finest features of Inventions One and Two. The whole contraption lowered a magnet onto the tiny clock part, picked it up, and swung it through the kitchen window into Ferguson's hand. He handed the clock part to Willard.

"Well," said Willard, "you finally invented something useful."

Ferguson looked at his Mom and smiled. She smiled back. They both knew that Invention Number Three would never have happened without Inventions Number One and Two.

UNLAWFUL TO PHOTOCOPY

1 Which best expresses the main idea of the story?

A   A boy disapproves of his brother's activities.
B   An inventive boy finds a use for his skill.
C   A family loses a piece of a kitchen clock.
D   A boy hopes to become a famous inventor.

2 Read this sentence from the story.

> On a table in Ferguson's bedroom was a contraption made of wooden sticks, cardboard tubes and rubber bands.

What does the word "contraption" mean?

A   something small   C   two words joined together
B   a patched-together machine   D   a type of trap

3 Read this sentence from the story.

> He knew that all famous inventors were scoffed at early in their careers.

What word means the opposite of "scoffed at"?

A   welcomed   C   criticized
B   praised   D   scolded

4 Read this sentence from the story.

> Ferguson peered out the apartment window.

Which word means the same as "peered"?

A   appeared   C   jumped
B   looked   D   shouted

5 In the story, the "fire escape" is

A   an outdoor staircase leading from the apartment
B   a type of fire engine used in large cities
C   a new invention by Ferguson Jones
D   a place where people store things in an apartment house

UNLAWFUL TO PHOTOCOPY

CHAPTER 6

LOOKING AT THE DETAILS

In the last chapter, you learned how to find the main idea of a reading. In this chapter, you will learn how to answer questions about finding details and relating those details to each other.

Let's begin by examining an informational reading. The passage below was written when basketball was celebrating its 100th birthday. It will provide a basis for the sample questions in this chapter.

CHILD LIFE
The Children's Own Magazine

April, May 2000   Vol. 7, Number 5

HAPPY BIRTHDAY, BASKETBALL!
by Charles Davis

It was the summer of 1891. Born in Canada in 1861, James Naismith had just become an instructor at the YMCA Training School in Springfield, Massachusetts. At that time, students played football in the fall and baseball in the spring. There were no winter sports. During winter months students at the YMCA were required to do one hour of exercising each day.

Naismith was given a challenge by his boss: to invent a new game. It had to be easy to learn and easy to play indoors during the winter. The game couldn't be rough or dangerous. Most important, it had to be fun and played to the highest standards of good sportsmanship.

CONTINUED

UNLAWFUL TO PHOTOCOPY

At first, James tried taking outdoor games the students knew and bringing them indoors. But indoor rugby and soccer were too rough to play in a small gym. People could get hurt. When his students played lacrosse in the gym, they broke the windows. With only a day left before he had to report the new game to his boss, James still hadn't come up with the right game.

So he started thinking. Why not take parts from different games and make a new one? From soccer, he chose the large ball. From lacrosse, he took the idea of a goal.

He decided to put the goal up high so it could not be easily defended. From football came the idea of passing the ball to move it down the court.

As he slept that night, he dreamed of the new game. The next morning, he wrote down thirteen rules. Then he went to look for something to use as goals.

James Naismith and his wife stand next to the peach basket first used as the game's goals.

He asked building repairman Pop Stebbins for two boxes, but Pop could not find any. "I have two peach baskets in the storeroom. Will they do?" Pop said. James took the baskets and tacked them to the jogging track along the gym's ten-foot-high balcony.

As the students entered the gym, James explained the rules to them. Then the world's first basketball game got under way. It was a little confusing at first. Nobody really knew the rules yet. When the game was over, the score was 1 to 0. All the students could talk about was how much fun the new game was.

In the years following that first game, basketball has changed in many ways. Bouncing the ball, or "dribbling," was added as another way to move the ball down the court. Peach baskets were replaced with metal baskets, but they still didn't have open bottoms until 1912.

UNLAWFUL TO PHOTOCOPY

CONTINUED ▶

Soon the game became the most popular activity at the YMCA. Today, it's one of the world's favorite games.

James Naismith died in 1939 at age 78. He would be pleased to see modern players soar through the air for a jam or thread a pass through the lane. But he'd be even happier to see them shaking hands as friends when the game ended.

The team that played the first game of basketball at the YMCA Training School. Naismith is in a business suit.

FINDING DETAILS

Some questions on the **Grade 4 English Language Arts Test** will simply ask you to recall a particular detail from the reading. You will have to remember that detail or find it in the reading to answer the question. Let's look at a sample question based on the article, "Happy Birthday, Basketball!"

1 What was James Naismith's job at the YMCA Training School at the time he invented basketball?

   A basketball player
   B athletic director
   C sports instructor
   D building repairman

EXPLAINING YOUR ANSWER

What is the answer? _____

In which paragraph did you find the answer? _____

UNLAWFUL TO PHOTOCOPY

To answer *finding detail questions*, you should know how to **scan** a reading selection for specific information.

SCANNING

When you scan, you read through a passage quickly to locate specific information. Think of scanning as a treasure hunt. You are searching through the reading to find a piece of buried treasure.

Here is a technique many good readers use:

★ Scan by looking for **key words**. For example, this question asks about James Naismith's job. Look for places in the reading where **James Naismith** or the **YMCA Training School** are mentioned.

★ Force your eyes to race along the page. The idea is not to read each sentence. Instead, only stop each time you see the key words **James Naismith** or **YMCA Training School**. If that sentence does not have the information you need, continue to scan the remainder of the text.

★ Once you locate the information you are looking for, you need to focus in and read that sentence or group of sentences more carefully.

To answer Question 1 on the previous page, first scan the reading passage. Sometimes, as in this particular question, the answer to a detail question will be found directly in one part of the text. In fact, the very first paragraph tells you that James Naismith had just become an instructor at the YMCA Training School when he invented basketball.

Let's continue with additional *detail questions* about the article, "Happy Birthday, Basketball!"

UNLAWFUL TO PHOTOCOPY

2 In what year was basketball first invented by Naismith?

A 1851   C 1921

B 1891   D 1951

To answer a question testing your recall of a particular detail in the reading, try the following strategy:

UNLOCKING THE ANSWER

First, see if you can simply recall the answer. Even if you can, it helps to check by looking through the passage. Identify any key words in the question that might "unlock" the answer. Then **scan** through the reading passage looking for those **key words**.

Sometimes, the answer to a *detail question* in the reading will be worded slightly differently from the way it appears in the question.

On occasion, you may need information from two or more places in the passage to answer the question. By piecing this information together, you will be able to answer the question.

Finally, look over the answer choices. Make sure that the answer you choose is supported by some detail, fact or example found in the reading. If you cannot find this support, your choice is probably incorrect.

Now try using this strategy to answer the following **detail question**.

3 Which games did Naismith attempt to play indoors before he invented basketball?

A rugby and lacrosse

B tennis and fencing

C football and baseball

D soccer and football

UNLAWFUL TO PHOTOCOPY

SEQUENCE QUESTIONS

Some questions ask how details are related. For example, a question could ask about the sequence or chronological order of events:

What happened *before* or *after* an event in the story?

Which event happened *first* or *last*?

Which is the correct order of events in the story?

This kind of question tests how well you understand the order of events in the reading passage. Let's try answering a *sequence question* about the article "Happy Birthday, Basketball!"

4 Which event in the article happened first?

   A Pop Stebbins brought out two peach baskets from the storeroom.
   B Students at the YMCA played the first basketball game.
   C Dribbling was added to the game of basketball.
   D Naismith wrote down 13 rules for the new game.

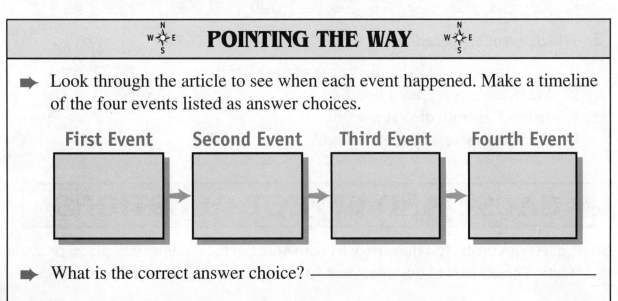

POINTING THE WAY

➡ Look through the article to see when each event happened. Make a timeline of the four events listed as answer choices.

First Event	Second Event	Third Event	Fourth Event

➡ What is the correct answer choice? —————————————

To answer a question about the sequence of events, try the steps listed on the next page:

UNLAWFUL TO PHOTOCOPY

UNLOCKING THE ANSWER

First, find the events listed in the question.

Next, pay attention to the order of those events. Remember, most writers present events in the order in which they have taken place. The author tells you if an event is out of sequence: for example, a character might remember something from the past.

★ Number the events in the margins of the reading or make a list of the order in which they happened.

★ Make a diagram, such as a timeline, showing the order of events in the story.

Finally, look over the answer choices. Pick the answer that states the correct order of events.

5 Which event happened last?

A   Dribbling was added to the game of basketball.
B   Metal baskets replaced beach baskets.
C   James Naismith died at age 78.
D   Baskets were given open bottoms.

CAUSE-AND-EFFECT QUESTIONS

Some questions on the test may ask **why** something in the reading took place, or about its **effects**. These kinds of questions test your understanding of **cause and effect**.

★ The **cause** of something is what made it happen. For example, if you turn on a light switch, you cause the light to go on. Questions asking for a cause often begin with the word *why*.

★ The **effect** of something is what happens as a result. The effect of your turning on the light switch is that the light goes on.

Unlawful to Photocopy

Often, key words in the reading will help you answer the question. These key words include: *why, because*, *as a result*, and *in order to*. Sometimes you will not find these key words in the reading, but it will still be clear that one event caused another.

If the question asks *why* something happened, look through the reading for a **cause**. Quite often something happens because of the actions of one or more individuals or characters.

Think about why these people acted as they did. The *reason why* someone did something often explains *why* it occurred. Always think about the motives or reasons of the people or characters involved when answering a question about why an event took place.

Now that you have an idea of what to look for, let's practice answering *cause-and-effect questions* about the article on basketball.

6 Why did James Naismith invent the game of basketball?

   A He was bored with the game of soccer.
   B His boss challenged him to invent a new game.
   C He disliked staying outdoors in winter.
   D His main job was to coach new and different games.

EXPLAINING YOUR ANSWER

What is the answer? _____

Identify which sentence in the passage backs up your answer.

_____

_____

UNLAWFUL TO PHOTOCOPY

Did you discover any special strategies for answering *cause-and-effect questions*? Here is a strategy often used by good readers for answering *cause-and-effect questions*.

UNLOCKING THE ANSWER

🔑 **First**, look over the question carefully. Does it ask for a cause or an effect?

🔑 **Next**, find the events the question asks about:

★ Use key words and other clues to find the cause of something. Think how a person's actions might have caused the event.

★ For effects, think about what happened because of that event. To decide why an event is important, think about its effects.

🔑 **Finally**, look over the answer choices to pick the best one.

Let's practice this strategy for answering *cause-and-effect questions*.

7   Why were Naismith's students unable to play outdoor sports in the gym at the YMCA?

A   The players became overheated too quickly.
B   The games were too rough for indoors.
C   The school had a rule against playing outdoor games inside.
D   The students voted against outdoor sports in the gym.

8   What caused Naismith to place the baskets ten feet high?

A   It allowed him to use peach baskets for the goals.
B   Ten-foot high-baskets could not be easily defended.
C   It would prevent players from damaging the baskets.
D   High baskets made passing the ball unnecessary.

UNLAWFUL TO PHOTOCOPY

COMPARE-AND-CONTRAST QUESTIONS

Compare-and-contrast questions ask you to compare two or more characters, persons, places, or things. Usually, the question will ask you how the items are similar or different.

9 Based on the article, what do the games of basketball and football have in common?

   A Both use baskets as goals.
   B Both require dribbling a ball.
   C Both allow the player with the ball to be tackled.
   D Both permit passing the ball to other team members.

EXPLAINING YOUR ANSWER

What is the answer? ———————— Explain why you picked that answer.

_____

_____

Sometimes it helps to make a **Venn diagram** to answer a *compare-and-contrast question*. To create one, draw two overlapping circles, ovals, or boxes. Write the characteristics common to the items you are comparing in the overlapping section. Put other characteristics or information unique to each item in the other part of each shape. For example:

FOOTBALL   BASKETBALL

- ball must cross over a goal line
- usually played outdoors

ball can be passed to other teammates

- ball must pass through a basket
- usually played indoors

Question 9 above asks how these two sports are alike. The Venn diagram shows what these two sports have in common: the passing of the ball to other teammates. Therefore, which do you think is the correct answer?

UNLAWFUL TO PHOTOCOPY

To answer a *compare-and-contrast question*, use the following steps:

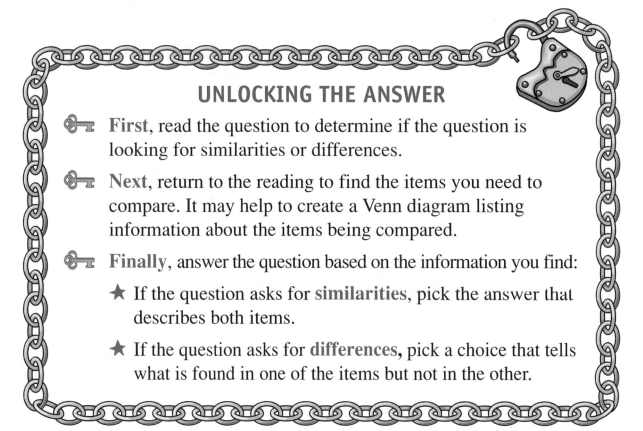

UNLOCKING THE ANSWER

First, read the question to determine if the question is looking for similarities or differences.

Next, return to the reading to find the items you need to compare. It may help to create a Venn diagram listing information about the items being compared.

Finally, answer the question based on the information you find:

★ If the question asks for **similarities**, pick the answer that describes both items.

★ If the question asks for **differences,** pick a choice that tells what is found in one of the items but not in the other.

SUPPORTING IDEAS WITH SPECIFIC DETAILS

A final type of *detail question* asks you to support an idea or a general statement from the reading with specific supporting details. This kind of question tests your ability to connect general statements to details in the reading.

Let's look at an example of this type of question:

10 Which information from the article best shows that Naismith was a creative instructor?

    A Naismith always followed his boss' orders.

    B Naismith thought about sports even while he slept.

    C Naismith borrowed ideas from different games to invent a new one.

    D Naismith felt rugby and soccer were too rough for indoor play.

UNLAWFUL TO PHOTOCOPY

EXPLAINING YOUR ANSWER

What is the answer? _____ Explain why you picked that answer.

_____

Think of this kind of question as asking you to pretend you are a lawyer in court. You tell the jury: "Ladies and gentlemen, Naismith was a creative instructor while working at the YMCA!" However, your opinion is not enough to persuade the jury. You must give **specific information** from the article to prove this general statement. To answer a question asking you to support a general statement or idea with information from the reading, try the following steps used by good readers:

UNLOCKING THE ANSWER

First, read the question and make sure you understand what it says. Does the question ask you to find facts, examples, or even specific sentences from the reading passage? Briefly look at the answer choices. Do any of them clearly support the general statement or idea in the question. *Which choice shows that Naismith was creative?*

Next, if you cannot answer the question just by reading the choices, then find the section of the reading that has the information you need. Read that section. See if it provides details supporting the statement or idea in the question.

Finally, based on the information you found in the passage, select the answer choice that best answers the question.

UNLAWFUL TO PHOTOCOPY

Now practice answering another question that asks you to support a statement with information from the reading. To answer the following question, use the strategy you just learned.

11 Which sentence from the article shows that the students at the YMCA enjoyed playing the very first basketball game?

A "Most important, it had to be fun and played to the highest standards of good sportsmanship."

B "As he slept that night, he dreamed of the new game."

C "Soon the game became the most popular activity at the YMCA."

D "All the students could talk about was how much fun the new game was."

PRACTICE EXERCISE

Read the following article and answer the questions that follow.

CHILD LIFE
The Children's Own Magazine

April, May 2000   Vol. 7, Number 5

ELIZABETH BLACKWELL

"Mother, I've finally decided on a career," announced twenty-four year old Elizabeth. "I'm going to study medicine."

Mrs. Blackwell accepted this statement calmly. "Are you sure, dear?" she asked. "Remember the bull's eye?"

"Oh, I remember all too well," thought Elizabeth. One day a teacher had brought the eye of a bull into class for a lesson on how the eye works. She remembered how upset she felt after seeing the eye. Her family had teased her about her *squeamishness* ever since that day.

Elizabeth Blackwell

CONTINUED ➡

UNLAWFUL TO PHOTOCOPY

"I'm sure, Mother," said Elizabeth, in a determined way. "I've been thinking about it and I've made up my mind. I'm going to be doctor."

Mrs. Blackwell did not argue. She knew Elizabeth had a strong spirit of determination. She thought Elizabeth was attracted to medicine because the mission seemed impossible. In 1845, a woman doctor was unheard of in America. No medical school would take in female students. Besides, Elizabeth had no money. But she did not let any of these things stop her.

First, Elizabeth found a position as a music teacher in a girls' school in North Carolina. After a year, she moved to South Carolina, where she continued to teach. There she had access to a doctor's library, where she read about medicine. She also kept saving her money. Elizabeth then moved to Philadelphia. She persuaded Dr. Warrington, a doctor, to let her observe him during the day at his medical practice.

With Dr. Warrington's help, she applied to medical schools in 1847. Some were polite, while others were hostile. But the replies were always the same —NO!

There was a small college in Geneva, New York — at the bottom of her list. Dr. Warrington suggested she try there. The head of the college decided to let the medical students themselves decide whether or not to admit a woman student. He didn't know that his rowdy students were in a playful mood that day. As a joke, they voted to admit Elizabeth to their school.

Blonde and pretty, Elizabeth finally had her chance. She overcame her squeamishness, attended every lecture, earned the respect of other students, and graduated at the top of her class in 1849.

In 1974, the U.S. Postal Service issued this stamp to honor Elizabeth Blackwell.

Far from being over, her troubles were just starting. While a degree from a two-year medical college might be enough for a man, she knew she would need more training to succeed. She sailed to London, then went to France for further study. While working at a Paris hospital, she had an accident that caused her to lose one eye. Now she was forced to give up her plans to study surgery.

Unlawful to Photocopy

CONTINUED

So she came back to America, where she opened a dispensary (*a kind of clinic*) in the slums of New York. Slowly, her patients began to accept her. Then her younger sister Emily graduated from medical school in Ohio, and came to help her.

On May 12, 1857, they opened the New York Infirmary for Women and Children. Hating the stark, bare look of hospital rooms, they furnished the hospital in a cheerful, homelike fashion. Elizabeth was the director, and Emily was the surgeon. The hospital was a great success. Later they opened their own medical school for women.

Elizabeth lived to be more than ninety. By sheer determination, she overcame all obstacles to make herself into a physician. In the process, she also opened the door for all women doctors who came after her.

1 What is the article mostly about?

  A the condition of American medical schools 150 years ago
  B a woman's determination to become America's first female doctor
  C the struggle of American women to win equal rights with men
  D a woman's attempt to overcome her squeamishness

2 What could also be a good title for the article?

  A A Squeamish Young Girl
  B America's First Woman Doctor
  C A Woman Opens a Hospital
  D Blackwell Returns to America

3 What does the word *squeamishness* in the third paragraph mean?

  A greed
  B illness
  C being easily sickened
  D being cold to others

4 Why did Elizabeth decide to teach in a music school?

  A She loved to sing and play music.
  B She wanted to help young and needy children.
  C She felt it might increase her chances of getting into a medical school.
  D She wanted to save money to pay for medical school.

UNLAWFUL TO PHOTOCOPY

5 Which statement from the story **best** illustrates Elizabeth's determination?

   A   *She remembered how upset she felt after seeing the eye.*
   B   *But she did not let any of these things stop her.*
   C   *Far from being over, her troubles were just starting.*
   D   *Hating the stark, bare look of hospital rooms, they furnished the hospital in a cheerful, homelike fashion.*

6 Based on the article, how were Elizabeth and her sister similar?

   A   Both were the same age.
   B   Both worked as music teachers.
   C   Both went to medical school.
   D   Both had lived in France.

7 What is the most likely reason why the U.S. Postal Service issued a stamp to honor Elizabeth Blackwell in 1947?

   A   She fought to overcome her squeamishness.
   B   She traveled more often than other women of her time.
   C   She was the first woman to earn a medical degree in the United States.
   D   She was a gifted and popular music teacher.

8 Which of these events in Elizabeth Blackwell's life occurred last?

   A   Elizabeth taught music in North Carolina.
   B   Elizabeth decided to become a doctor.
   C   Elizabeth became America's first woman to earn a medical degree.
   D   Elizabeth established an infirmary in New York City.

9 In the last paragraph, what does the author mean by writing that Elizabeth "opened the door for all women doctors who came after her"?

   A   At the hospital, Elizabeth often held the door open for other doctors.
   B   After Elizabeth's success, American women gained the right to vote.
   C   Elizabeth's achievement allowed other women to become doctors.
   D   American women who wanted to study medicine had to attend Elizabeth's New York Infirmary.

In this chapter, you learned how to answer five types of detail questions. For each one, there was a separate Unlocking the Answer. Can you see any similarities in how you approach each of these different types of questions?

UNLAWFUL TO PHOTOCOPY

CHAPTER 7

QUESTIONS ABOUT STORIES

Some questions on the **English Language Arts Test** will ask you about the *setting*, *characters*, *plot*, or *theme* of a story. In this chapter, you will learn how to answer these kinds of questions. Let's begin by reading a story similar to those on the actual test. The rest of the chapter will use this story as a basis for sample questions.

Highlights
for Children
A MAGAZINE FOR CHILDREN

September, 2001   Volume 56, Number 9

THE RECITAL
by Kathleen Benner Duble

"Hannah?" Mama said. "Are you all right?"

Hannah nodded yes. But it wasn't true. Since this morning her stomach had been doing flips like that day on the water slide when it kept going faster and faster and wouldn't slow down. When she had reached the bottom, she became sick in front of millions of people. Thinking of this made Hannah feel even sicker.

"You're not nervous, are you?" Mama said. Hannah shook her head no.

CONTINUED →

UNLAWFUL TO PHOTOCOPY

70

"Why would she be scared?" Mary piped up. "She only has to play 'Twinkle, Twinkle, Little Star.' It's so easy I never practice it anymore. Besides, I'll be playing it with her. I'm the one who should be scared."

At the mention of "Twinkle," Hannah felt her stomach turn again. She thought of the piano waiting at Mrs. Johnson's studio, and her mouth suddenly felt dry and sticky. Mary picked up her violin and began to play. It sounded beautiful to Hannah. It was something that would be too hard for her to play.

"I should be nervous," Mary said, "I have to play three pieces tonight. But I'm not scared."

Hannah knew Mary was not scared. Mary was never scared. Hannah wished she were more like Mary. Hannah stared at her own white blouse, dark skirt, white tights, and black shoes. She felt like a zebra.

Papa came into the room and scooped up Mary. "So, it's the big night, is it? I can't wait to hear my little musicians play." He grinned at Hannah. Hannah forced herself to smile back.

Papa hugged her against him, still holding Mary. "To the car," he said, "and on to Mrs. Johnson's studio."

Backstage, Hannah's hands were cold and damp. She felt on edge. All around, students were tuning their instruments. Hannah peeked through the closed curtains at the stage. The stage looked huge. The piano looked as if it could open its lid and eat her.

"Places, everyone!" called Mrs. Johnson. Mary danced into line behind Hannah and the other younger children.

Mary put her hand in Hannah's and squeezed it tight. "It'll be all right," she said softly. Weakly, Hannah squeezed back.

The curtain opened. One child played, then another. Soon, Hannah heard Mrs. Johnson announce her name and Mary's name. Slowly she walked on to the stage with Mary behind her. Hannah's legs felt weak. The lights were bright.

Unlawful to Photocopy

CONTINUED

Quickly, Hannah walked to the piano. Mary stood by her, and they bowed. There was clapping. Again, Hannah felt an awful taste in her mouth. When the clapping stopped, Hannah slid onto the piano bench. Mary put her violin to her chin and smiled at Hannah.

Mary and Hannah began to play. She thought about playing and nothing else. Suddenly, Hannah heard something odd. Mary was not playing "Twinkle." Hannah didn't know what Mary was playing. Hannah couldn't believe Mary was making a mess out of "Twinkle."

Hannah glanced at Mary. Her face was white, and her hands were trembling on the violin. Then Hannah realized that Mary had forgotten the notes, and was now scared.

"I should have practiced," Mary thought, almost crying. Hannah began whispering the notes to Mary — A, A, E, E, F-sharp …. Slowly, Mary hit the notes in time with Hannah's playing. When they finished, they finished together.

The clapping was loud in Hannah's ears. When they bowed, Hannah took Mary's hand. Mary's hand was damp and cold, but Hannah's hand was dry and warm. Backstage, Mary didn't say a word, but ran off to be with her friends.

"Were you nervous?" someone asked Mary. "Who, me?" said Mary, "I'm never scared."

Just then, Mary turned and caught Hannah's eye. Mary smiled, and Hannah smiled. Hannah would never tell. Mary was her sister. Deep inside Hannah felt comforted knowing Mary, too, could be scared.

QUESTIONS ABOUT THE STORY SETTING

The **setting** is *where* and *when* the story takes place. A story may actually have more than one setting. It could begin in one place and end in another. Questions on the setting of a story will usually ask you to identify the time or place of some part of the story.

UNLAWFUL TO PHOTOCOPY

The following is an example of a question about the setting of a story.

1 Where are the characters at the beginning of the story?

    A at a piano recital

    B in Hannah and Mary's house

    C in Mrs. Johnson's studio

    D in a car on the way to the recital

EXPLAINING YOUR ANSWER

What is the answer? _____

Which paragraph helped you to answer this? _____

For questions that ask you to *identify* the *time* or *place* of a story, try the following approach:

UNLOCKING THE ANSWER

First, look for clues in the story about *when* and *where* it takes place. These clues are often found at the beginning of the story. Remember that a story may be set in more than one time and place. The setting of the story often changes as the story unfolds.

If the setting is not described directly, it may be possible to guess at the setting from the descriptions, actions, or speech of the characters.

Finally, if you do not find information about the setting of the story at the beginning, scan through the story to find more details. Then choose the answer that best indicates the time and place you found.

Let's apply what you just learned to answer another question about the setting.

2 Where does the recital take place?

    A at Hannah's house   **C** in a local concert hall

    B at Ms. Johnson's studio   **D** the school auditorium

Some questions may also ask you to explain why the setting of a story is *important*:

3 Why is it important that the story ends at the recital?

    A Mary likes performing in public.

    B Hannah discovers that Mary is also nervous while performing.

    C The recital reminds Hannah of the water slide.

    D The recital shows the importance of Mrs. Johnson to the story.

To answer this question, think how the setting influences events in the story. For example, how does either the time or place of the story shape what happens? Choose the answer that best describes how the setting helps make events happen.

QUESTIONS ABOUT THE CHARACTERS

Sometimes, you may need to answer questions about the characters of a story or some other literary reading.

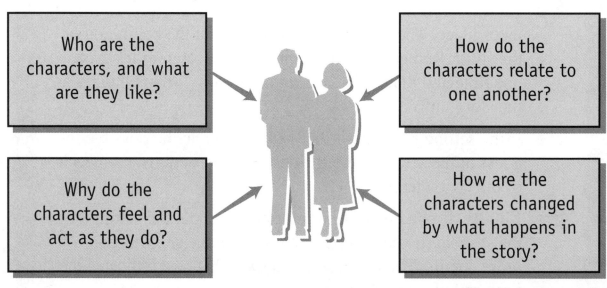

Who are the characters, and what are they like?

How do the characters relate to one another?

Why do the characters feel and act as they do?

How are the characters changed by what happens in the story?

When you read a story, it often helps to circle or underline the names of important characters when they are first mentioned. Focus on the **main characters**. Try to form a picture in your mind of what each character is like.

UNLAWFUL TO PHOTOCOPY

4 Which word **best** describes how Hannah's sister, Mary, felt before going to the piano recital?

A   tired

B   worried

C   confident

D   bored

EXPLAINING YOUR ANSWER

What is the answer? _____ Explain why you selected that answer.

_____

The answer to this question can be found by scanning the reading to find Mary's actions before going to the recital. The first paragraph on page 71 gives a clue to Mary's feelings. She says she is not scared. Here are some strategies to help you answer questions about the characters of a story:

UNLOCKING THE ANSWER

🔑 **First**, study the question. Be sure you understand what it asks.

🔑 Scan the reading to find information the question asks for.

★ If the question asks for a *description* of a character, find places in the reading where the character is described.

★ If the question asks how the character *thinks* or *acts* at a *specific time*, go to that part of the story to find the answer.

★ If the question asks how the character is *changed* by an event in the story, find that event in the story. Reread that part of the story to see how the character is changed.

🔑 Sometimes the information you need may not be stated directly in the reading. For example:

★ You may have to decide how a character *thinks* or *feels* based on how he or she *acts* in the story.

★ You may have to decide how a character is *changed* by an event based on how that character *acts afterwards*.

UNLAWFUL TO PHOTOCOPY

Now, let's practice answering questions about the characters of a story.

5 Look at these pictures of a girl's face.

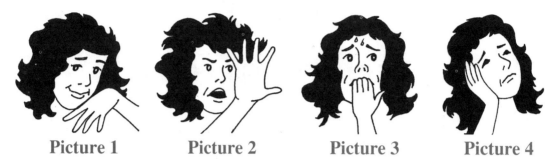

Picture 1   Picture 2   Picture 3   Picture 4

Which picture best shows how Hannah felt when her sister mentioned she would be playing "Twinkle, Twinkle, Little Star"?

A Picture 1   C Picture 3
B Picture 2   D Picture 4

To answer question 5, you need to scan the story to remind yourself how Hannah felt. The beginning paragraphs show that Hannah is nervous. Hannah's stomach is turning, and her mouth is dry and sticky. She is clearly worried when she thinks about the recital later that day. The best answer is therefore C. Picture 3 shows someone who is obviously feeling nervous.

6 What does Hannah do to help her sister Mary at the recital?

A She holds her violin.
B She squeezes Mary's hand.
C She helps Mary to practice.
D She whispers musical notes to her.

This question asks how a character acts. To find the correct answer, you should reread that part of the selection that tells about what the question asks for. A few paragraphs before the end of the story, we read how the two sisters behave at the recital. Here you will find the specific line that describes how Hannah helps her sister Mary during the performance — *"Hannah began whispering the notes to Mary."*

UNLAWFUL TO PHOTOCOPY

7 How is Hannah changed by what happened at the recital?

  A   She wishes to give up playing the piano.
  B   She refuses to ever perform with her sister again.
  C   She realizes others can be nervous too.
  D   She wants to learn how to play the violin.

> This question looks at how a character is changed by an event in the story. In order to answer this question, you need to review events *before*, *during* and *after* the recital. If you compare the last paragraphs of the story to the beginning, you can see how Hannah is changed by events at the recital.
>
> *What do you think is the best answer choice?* ——

8 How does Mary view her performance with Hannah at the recital?

  A   She believes she played well.
  B   She realizes that she should have practiced.
  C   She thinks the recital began too early.
  D   She realizes the song was more difficult than she thought.

> Here the question asks how a character views events in the story. Reread that part of the story that describes Mary's thoughts **during the recital**. She tells her friends one thing but gives Hanna a look meaning something entirely different.
>
> *What do you think is the best answer?* ——

QUESTIONS ABOUT THE PLOT

You know that the **plot** is the series of events that take place in a story. Generally, the main characters face some problem they must solve. This problem is what moves the story along. Questions about plot will often focus on the central or main problem of the story. They may ask you:

- to identify the central problem faced by the story characters
- to tell how these events help the characters solve the central problem
- to recognize important events in the story

UNLAWFUL TO PHOTOCOPY

IDENTIFYING THE CENTRAL PROBLEM

One type of question about the plot will ask you to identify the *main problem* of the story.

UNLOCKING THE ANSWER

To answer this kind of question, use the following steps:

🔑 **First**, read through the story to determine the major problem the characters face. Often it is presented early in the reading. Try to state this problem in a sentence.

🔑 **Next**, look carefully at the main events in the story. See if most of these events influence the ability of the characters to solve the central problem. If they do not, you may not have stated the problem correctly. For example, many events and details in "The Recital" have to do with Hannah's being nervous.

🔑 **Finally**, look at the answer choices. Pick the one that best describes the central problem.

Apply these steps to answer the following question about "The Recital."

9 What is the main problem of the story?

　A　Mary does not like to practice violin.
　B　Hannah is nervous about performing at a recital.
　C　Hannah is jealous of her sister Mary.
　D　Mary refuses to perform with her younger sister.

RELATING PLOT EVENTS

Some questions about the plot will ask you **why** certain story events happen or the order of events in the story. Answer these questions just as you would any other question relating to details.

UNLAWFUL TO PHOTOCOPY

SOLVING THE CENTRAL PROBLEM

You might also be asked how the main characters **solve** the central problem of the story.

10 How does Hannah deal with her nervousness?

    A She helps Mary by telling her the notes.

    B She gives up playing a musical instrument.

    C She joins a sports team in school.

    D She takes a long walk with her sister.

EXPLAINING YOUR ANSWER

What is the answer? _____ Explain why you selected that answer.

_____

To answer questions about how the main problem or conflict of the story is resolved, try this strategy:

UNLOCKING THE ANSWER

First, see if you can clearly identify the main problem or conflict faced by the main characters.

Then, look through the events of the story to see how the main character or characters deal with the central problem. Do they learn to accept it, or do they solve it in some way? Think about how the characters are *different* at the end of the story from how they were at the beginning.

Finally, look over the answer choices. Choose the one that best describes how the problem is solved.

UNLAWFUL TO PHOTOCOPY

QUESTIONS ABOUT THE THEME

A **theme** is any underlying message or lesson that the story teaches. The theme is what is universal about the story — how it applies to each of us. At other times, you have to figure out the story's theme. Often the theme does not become clear until the end of the story.

UNLOCKING THE ANSWER

A *theme question* will usually appear as:
★ *What is the theme of the story?*
★ *What lesson does a character learn in the story?*

It may help to think about a general message the story has that you could apply to your own life. Ask yourself:
★ What lesson can I learn from this story?
★ What advice does the author give to the reader?

Finally, select the answer choice closest to the theme or lesson you have identified.

Let's see how well you can answer a question asking about the theme of the story.

11 What is the main lesson that Hannah learns in the story?

A   Never show weakness to another member of the family.
B   Everyone experiences things that scare them sometimes.
C   If something makes you scared, you should avoid it.
D   Teachers seldom understand how young people feel.

EXPLAINING YOUR ANSWER

What is the answer? _____ Explain why you selected that answer.

_____

UNLAWFUL TO PHOTOCOPY

PRACTICE EXERCISE

Read the excerpt below. It is from the first chapter of the book *Josefina Learns a Lesson* by Valerie Tripp. Then answer the questions that follow.

"LIGHT AND SHADOW"

"Mariá Josefina Montoya!" said Tía [*aunt*] Dolores happily. "How beautiful you look!" Josefina blushed and smiled at her aunt. "Gracias," [*thank you*] she said. She smoothed the long skirt of her new dress with both hands. The cotton material felt soft and light. Josefina rose up on her toes and spun, just for the sheer pleasure of it. She was very proud of her dress, which she had just finished hemming. She had never had a dress made in this elegant, new, high-waisted style before.

Tía Dolores had given Josefina and each of her sisters some material. Josefina's material was a pretty yellow, with narrow stripes and tiny berries on it.

She had cut her material carefully, the way Mamá had taught her. Then stitch by tiny stitch, she had sewn her dress together all by herself. Now, as she spun around, the flames in the fireplace cast a pattern of light and shadow swooping across the dress like a flock of fluttering birds.

Josefina stopped spinning and sighed with peaceful contentment. It was a rainy evening in October. Josefina and her three older sisters, Ana, Francisca, and Clara, were sewing in front of the fire in the family *sala* [*large room*]. Tía Dolores was helping them. They were glad of the fire's warmth and cheerful brightness. A steady rain was falling outside, but inside it was cozy. The thick, whitewashed *adobe walls* [*made of earth mixed with straw and water*] kept out the cold and took on a rosy glow from the firelight.

Tía Dolores sat next to Clara. "Don't use such a long thread in your needle," she advised Clara gently. "It might tangle." Josefina grinned. "Remember, Clara?" she said. "Mamá used to say, 'If you make

UNLAWFUL TO PHOTOCOPY

CONTINUED ▶

your thread too long, the devil will catch on to the end of it.'"

All the sisters smiled and nodded, and Tía Dolores said, "I remember your Mamá saying that to me when we were young girls learning to sew!"

Tía Dolores was smiling. But Josefina saw that her eyes were sad, and she knew that Tía Dolores was missing Mamá. Tía Dolores was Mamá's sister. Mamá had died more than a year ago. Josefina and her sisters thought of Mamá every day, with

longing and love. The girls tried to do their chores the way Mamá had taught them. They tried to be as respectful, hardworking, and obedient as she would have wished them to be. Every day, they recalled her wise and funny sayings and songs. And every day, they remembered her in their prayers.

The first year after Mamá's death, the four girls had struggled to run the household. Then, at the end of the summer, Tía Dolores had come to visit. She was on her way home to Santa Fe from Mexico City, where she had been living for ten years. During her visit, the girls realized how much they needed someone like her — to help them and teach them as Mamá used to do. Tía Dolores kindly agreed to come live on the *rancho* for a while. She went to Santa Fe to see her parents for a month. But she kept her promise and returned to the *rancho* with her servant Teresita to help with the harvest. Tía Dolores had been back for two weeks now, and Josefina was glad.

1   Where does this scene take place?

   A   in a sewing class
   B   in the *sala* of an *adobe* house
   C   in a city market
   D   in a school in New Mexico

2   The fireplace is important to the story because it

   A   represents Josefina's mother to the young girls
   B   almost burns Josefina
   C   gives the sisters warmth and brightness on a dreary day
   D   is used by Tía Dolores to cook family meals

Unlawful to Photocopy

3 How do the four sisters feel about Tía Delores?

A   They resent their aunt's interference in their lives.

B   They feel their aunt should have died instead of their mother.

C   They are happy to have their aunt help out after their mother's death.

D   They dislike their aunt for trying to replace their mother.

4 What is the main problem in the story?

A   The family has to overcome the mother's death.

B   It is difficult for them to obtain clothing.

C   There is not enough food from the harvest.

D   The sisters resent their aunt's coming to live with them.

5 Which of the following events took place first?

A   Tía Delores gave the four sisters material to make dresses.

B   Josefina's mother died.

C   Tía Delores visited the family on her way home from Mexico City.

D   Josefina finished her new dress.

6 Which phrase from the story describes how Josefina and her sisters feel about their mother?

A   "peaceful contentment"

B   "longing and love"

C   "sheer pleasure"

D   "cheerful brightness"

7 Why did Tía Delores come for a visit at the end of the summer?

A   She wanted to see her sister's grave.

B   She was on her way home from Mexico City.

C   She knew her sister's family needed her help.

D   She wanted to experience life on a *rancho*.

8 What is an important lesson the four sisters learn in the story?

A   Young people often need the guidance of an adult.

B   Sewing is a useful way to pass the time.

C   Close relatives are rarely helpful to family members.

D   Past memories are best forgotten.

UNLAWFUL TO PHOTOCOPY

CHAPTER 8

GOING BEYOND THE READING

Some questions on the **Grade 4 English Language Arts Test** will examine your ability to go beyond a basic understanding of the reading and to make connections with what you already know. These questions may ask you:

To draw conclusions	To make predictions	To separate fact from opinion

To recognize an author's purpose or point of view	To locate information

In this chapter, you will learn how to answer questions that ask you to go beyond the reading. Read the following story about a girl, her neighbor, and her seeing-eye dog. This story will provide a basis for the practice questions in this chapter.

Highlights
for Children

September, 2001   Volume 56, Number 9

The Mystery of the Unfriendly Neighbor
By Diane Burns

For courage, my fingers cling to the harness on Chó's broad back as we pass my neighbor's fence. Walking by Mr. Groll's yard is the best part of our morning walk … and also the worst.

CONTINUED

UNLAWFUL TO PHOTOCOPY

It is the best part because the roses talk to us. "Good morning, Chó," whisper the rose scents to my guide dog's nose. Other roses shout to me, "Hello, Mai!" with a smell that bursts bold as firecrackers. Now comes the worst part — the unfriendly shape nearby that shades us: Mr. Groll. As usual, friendly Chó thumps her tail. But Chó is just a dog; how can she know that this neighbor does not like me at all?

"Hello, Mr. Groll." I greet him as I do every morning.

And like every other morning, he does not answer me. But I know he's there, watching behind his fence. He sounds out of breath, and the creaky gate swings nervously in his hand.

Maybe he's afraid of me because I'm blind. Disabilities scare grown-ups sometimes. Then I remember: yesterday I heard him playing checkers with my friend Jimmy, who's in a wheelchair. Chó and I march on, and my thoughts keep step. Why does Mr. Groll ignore me? He likes roses. I like roses. Why can't two people who like roses like each other? It's a mystery to me.

Chó and I stop for a moment near the rosebushes while I think. Papa has told me that some folks do not like people from faraway places. Does this solve the mystery? Maybe Mr. Groll does not like Vietnamese neighbors.

No, that can't be it. Every Saturday Mr. Groll and my big brother, Lien, help each other with yard work. They are friends. Well, then, I wonder, why won't he talk to *me*?

The toe of my shoe scuffs the sidewalk, and I think, maybe he doesn't like girls. The sidewalk hums beneath my feet as a skateboard zooms by. "Hello, Mai and Chó!" Jana hollers. "Hi, Mr. Groll."

UNLAWFUL TO PHOTOCOPY

CONTINUED ▶

I wait. If Mr. Groll ignores Jana, then the mystery is solved. But his voice calls out, "Hello, Jana!" The sound of it twists my heart. Now I know something I didn't know before: some people who can see can be blind. Sometimes, their hearts don't see any better than my eyes do. And I also know that unfriendly Mr. Groll likes Jimmy. And Lien. And Jana. But not me and Chó.

Me and Chó! Maybe I know why Mr. Groll doesn't talk to me! "Down," I command, releasing Chó's harness as she flops to the ground. I attach her harness to a post, and feel my way along the fence.

The gate squeaks open. "Mai! Be careful!" Mr. Groll's startled voice steadies my courage while his hand steadies my elbow.

"You can solve my mystery," I stammer. I take a deep breath. "It isn't because I'm blind that you don't like me. Or because I am a girl from Vietnam." I sigh. "It's Chó who scares you when we walk by. That's why you are shaking even now."

His large voice shrinks. "I like you, Mai. And Chó, too. But up close, Chó scares my words away." His breath sounds thin. "A German shep-herd is a very big dog," he says in a voice that tells me he thinks I will laugh at him. But being scared isn't funny. I have learned that myself. So I tell him, "Your fear of Chó may be big, but friendship is bigger. We will help. Come with me."

I hear a smile in Mr. Groll's voice. "OK," he says, "I trust you, my friend." Friend, he called me. We are friends!

I lead him back to Chó, and tell Mr. Groll how gentle Chó is. Then I take his hand and guide it to Chó's head. Hesitantly, Mr. Groll pets Chó's ears. Friendly Chó thumps her tail. And now that the mystery is solved, our new friendship can begin.

Unlawful to Photocopy

DRAWING CONCLUSIONS

Some questions on the test may ask you to **draw conclusions** from details in a story or informational reading. A *conclusion* is a general judgment you can make based on details in the reading. To answer a *conclusion question*, you'll need two things — your "thinking hat" and an ability to reason.

Conclusion questions really stretch your ability to figure things out. In these kinds of questions, the answer will *not* be found directly in the reading. Instead, like a good detective, you need to look carefully at "clues" in the reading. These details or "clues" will point to the correct answer choice.

To see how this works, pretend that you have an older sister. She and her friend have been playing softball in front of your house. Suddenly, the front doorbell

rings. You open the door and your next-door neighbor is standing there, holding a softball in his hand. He says the windshield on his car has been broken.

EXPLAINING YOUR ANSWER

What conclusion would you draw from this situation? _____

_____

What led you to that conclusion? _____

_____

As you can see, *drawing a conclusion* requires going beyond what is written. You have to consider details in the reading and see where they point to. No one told you that your sister and her friend broke the car windshield. However, you can probably guess that this is what happened.

UNLAWFUL TO PHOTOCOPY

Now let's look at a *conclusion question* about the story you just read.

1 From the information in the story, the reader can conclude that

   A Mr. Groll does not like people with disabilities.

   B Mr. Groll does not like people from Vietnam.

   C Mr. Groll is a friendly person.

   D Mr. Groll owns a large dog.

> From information in the story, choices **A** and **B** can be eliminated. Mai thinks Mr. Groll dislikes people with disabilities, but recalls that he plays with Jimmy, who is in a wheelchair. She also thinks Mr. Groll does not like Vietnamese people, but remembers he helps Lien, her brother. In the story, we learn that Mr. Groll is scared of large dogs like German shepherds. It is reasonable to conclude that he does not own one, eliminating choice **D**. We can conclude that Mr. Groll is friendly — he is friends with Jimmy, Lien, Jana, and even Mai when she approaches him without her dog. Therefore, choice **C** is the correct answer.

To answer a *conclusion question*, you should take the following steps:

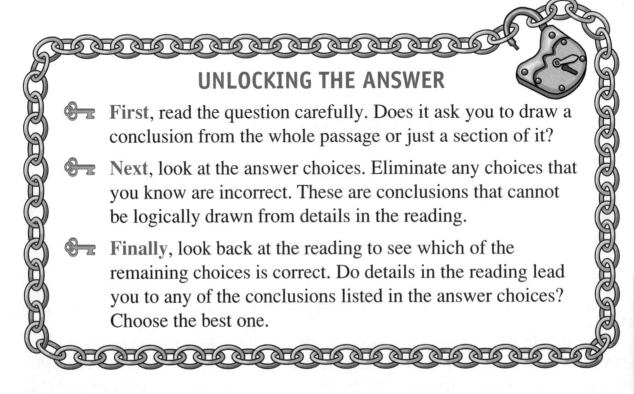

UNLOCKING THE ANSWER

First, read the question carefully. Does it ask you to draw a conclusion from the whole passage or just a section of it?

Next, look at the answer choices. Eliminate any choices that you know are incorrect. These are conclusions that cannot be logically drawn from details in the reading.

Finally, look back at the reading to see which of the remaining choices is correct. Do details in the reading lead you to any of the conclusions listed in the answer choices? Choose the best one.

UNLAWFUL TO PHOTOCOPY

Now you try answering a *conclusion question* based on the same story.

2 What conclusion can be drawn from the story about Mai's dog, Chó?

  A Chó does not like the smell of roses.
  B Chó is afraid of Mr. Groll.
  C Chó is a very obedient dog.
  D Chó is still only a puppy.

PREDICTION QUESTIONS

Good readers try to predict what will happen next when they read. As they continue reading, they see if their predictions come true. Even when the story or informational reading reaches an end, they think about what might happen next.

Prediction questions test your ability to apply what you have learned from a reading to new situations. *Prediction questions* might appear as:

What is likely to happen next?

What is a character from the story likely to do in the future?

For example, look at the following *prediction question*:

3 How is Mr. Groll likely to change in the future?

  A He will give up planting roses.
  B He will stop playing with Jimmy.
  C He will buy a large dog.
  D He will say hello to Mai.

EXPLAINING YOUR ANSWER

From the reading, we learn that Mr. Groll is afraid of Mai's dog. However, Mai guides Mr. Groll's hand across Chó to show how gentle her dog is.

Based on this, how do you think Mr. Groll might change in the future?

_____

_____

What do you think is the correct answer? _____

UNLAWFUL TO PHOTOCOPY

To answer a *prediction question*, here is a strategy you might use:

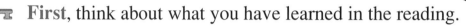

UNLOCKING THE ANSWER

First, think about what you have learned in the reading.

Next, use what you have learned to **predict** what is likely to happen in a new or different situation. The answer must be in keeping with information in the story. Some answer choices may seem to make sense, but if the answer does not logically follow from the main conflict in the story, it is probably incorrect.

For example, choice **D** in question 3 is unlikely since Mr. Groll still has a strong fear of large dogs. However, because of the actions of Mai, he has become less afraid of Chó and will probably greet Mai in the future.

Finally, select the answer choice closest to your prediction.

Now you try to answer a *prediction question*:

4 If the story were to continue, what would be most likely to happen next?

A   Mai's father would scold Mr. Groll for ignoring his daughter.
B   Mr. Groll would move away from the neighborhood.
C   Mai and Mr. Groll would become better friends.
D   Mai would get a new guide dog to lead her.

FACT-AND-OPINION QUESTIONS

Do you know the difference between a **fact** and an **opinion**? Some questions on the **Grade 4 English Language Arts Test** may ask you to identify a fact or an opinion.

Unlawful to Photocopy

FACT

A **fact** is a statement that can be shown to be correct or true. "The table is red" is a statement of fact. People can look at the table to see if it is red. Other facts can be checked by using other sources. Suppose someone tells you that there was a fire yesterday at 42 Maple Lane. You can look in the newspaper, call the fire department, or even visit Maple Lane to check if there really was a fire.

CHECKING YOUR UNDERSTANDING

Write a **fact** based on something you did today. _____

_____

OPINION

An **opinion** is a statement of personal feelings or beliefs. Words such as *think*, *feel*, *probably*, and *believe* often show that a statement is an opinion. This statement is an opinion: "I believe Rudy Giuliani was the best mayor of New York City." No one can prove Giuliani was the best mayor. The statement just tells us the writer's personal belief.

Writers often make statements that look like facts although they are actually opinions. For example, "Our soap cleans the best!" Writers do this to sound more convincing. Ask yourself: Can this be checked, or is it an expression of the writer's beliefs?

CHECKING YOUR UNDERSTANDING

Write an **opinion** based on something you did today. _____

_____

UNLAWFUL TO PHOTOCOPY

Let's practice answering a *fact-and-opinion question*. Read the letter below to the Director of the American Museum of Natural History in New York City about a possible exhibit.

Director, American Museum of Natural History
81st Street and Central Park West
New York, New York 10024

Dear Director,

I have recently read that the American Museum of Natural History is thinking about having a special exhibit in honor of Albert Einstein. I am writing to say that I think this would be an excellent idea.

Einstein's theories changed many of our scientific ideas. One of his theories stated that time and space are related. How fast time passes is based on how fast something moves. At the speed of light, Einstein said, time stands still. Einstein also said that things could be changed into immense amounts of energy. All this may seem very strange, but experiments have shown that Einstein was right. His theories led to the development of the atomic bomb and nuclear energy.

As one of the greatest scientists of all time, Einstein surely deserves to have a special exhibit at the museum. The exhibit should focus on explaining his theories and all the wonderful discoveries and inventions his theories have led to.

Sincerely,

Cedric Williams

Now that you have finished reading this letter, answer the question that follows.

5 Which of the following expresses an opinion of the author?

A *Einstein's theories changed many of our scientific ideas.*
B *This theory states that time and space are related.*
C *At the speed of light, Einstein said, time stands still.*
D *As one of the greatest scientists of all times, Einstein surely deserves to have a special exhibit at the museum.*

UNLAWFUL TO PHOTOCOPY

Check the box to show which statements are fact or opinion statements.

	Fact	Opinion
1. Abraham Lincoln was the sixteenth President of the United States.	☐	☐
2. Some Mexican food are spicy.	☐	☐
3. The N.Y. Stock Exchange is located in Manhattan.	☐	☐
4. Fourth graders have too much homework.	☐	☐

Exaggerations. Writers sometimes exaggerate. When you exaggerate, you stretch something beyond the facts. For example, a fisherman may have caught a few flounder when fishing. He would be exaggerating if he told his friends he caught a dozen.

When you read an informational text, you should be aware of which statements are *facts*, *opinions*, and *exaggerations*. A text is more believable if it provides accurate facts to support its main ideas.

AN AUTHOR'S PURPOSE OR VIEWPOINT

Some questions may ask you about an author's purpose. Authors generally have one of the following purposes in mind when they write:

★ **To Inform.** Informational, nonfiction readings — such as articles — are usually written to provide readers with facts and ideas. The author wants to give readers information about the world.

★ **To Entertain.** Literary texts — such as stories, poems, and plays — are written to entertain readers. Stories with interesting characters and lively plots are fun to read, even though they often have an underlying lesson.

★ **To Persuade.** Some authors write to persuade readers to form a particular opinion or to act in a certain way. Letters to the editor, speeches, and essays are all forms of persuasive writing.

★ **To Express Feelings.** Some authors write to express their deepest feelings. Many essays, poems, and stories express strong emotions.

UNLAWFUL TO PHOTOCOPY

Look at the next question based on the story you read in this chapter.

6 Why did the author **most likely** write this story?

    A to persuade readers to be kind to people with disabilities
    B to entertain readers with a story about overcoming misunderstanding
    C to inform people about the importance of seeing-eye dogs
    D to express her feelings about people from other countries

To answer questions about the author's purpose, try using the following strategy:

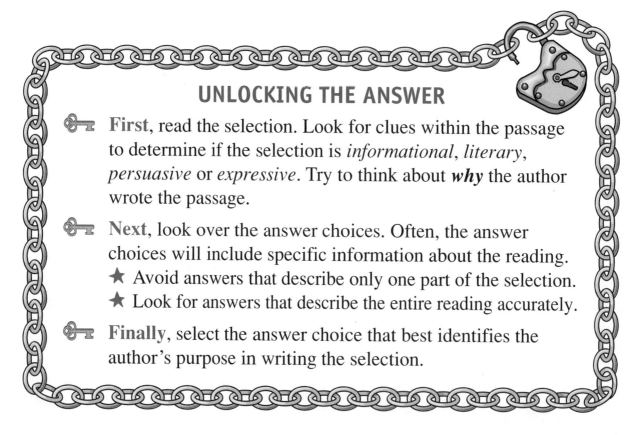

UNLOCKING THE ANSWER

First, read the selection. Look for clues within the passage to determine if the selection is *informational*, *literary*, *persuasive* or *expressive*. Try to think about **why** the author wrote the passage.

Next, look over the answer choices. Often, the answer choices will include specific information about the reading.
★ Avoid answers that describe only one part of the selection.
★ Look for answers that describe the entire reading accurately.

Finally, select the answer choice that best identifies the author's purpose in writing the selection.

Another type of question asks for the author's viewpoint and how that affects the passage. Questions about an author's viewpoint will often ask how the author's attitude toward the subject influences what he or she writes. You can see this by looking at the question on the next page.

UNLAWFUL TO PHOTOCOPY

7 How do the author's views influence the way Mai is described?

A   The author shows Mai as someone who seeks to understand others.

B   The author describes Mai as often scared without good reason.

C   The author portrays Mai as a girl with foolish ideas.

D   The author criticizes Mai for her lack of understanding.

UNLOCKING THE ANSWER

First, review the selection to determine the author's point of view. There are certain questions you can ask yourself to help you discover an author's viewpoint:

★ Does the author like what he or she describes?

★ Does the author sympathize with any of the characters?

★ Is the author happy, disappointed, or angry about what he or she is writing about?

Next, think about how the author's attitude influences what he or she writes. For example, if a writer thinks that a person or event is bad, the author may use negative words to describe that person or event.

Finally, pick the answer that best identifies the author's viewpoint.

LOCATING INFORMATION

As a fourth grader, you should be able to use the table of contents and index to locate information in a book. Some questions on the test may examine your skill at using these two tools. Let's take a look at a table of contents and an index from *A Guide to the American Museum of Natural History*.

UNLAWFUL TO PHOTOCOPY

Books and magazines usually begin with a **table of contents**. It shows the chapters of the book and the pages where they are found. The **index** is located in the back of the book. It lists topics and people in alphabetical order and shows the pages of the book where those topics appear.

Now try answering some questions on locating information based on the table of contents and index above.

8 In which chapter of *A Guide to the American Museum of Natural History* would you look for information about how the museum was started?

A Chapter 1   C Chapter 3
B Chapter 2   D Chapter 4

9 In which page of *A Guide to the American Museum of Natural History* would you look to find information on the sapphire called the Star of India?

A page 20   C page 57
B page 55   D page 59

10 In which chapter and pages of the guide would you find information about galleries located outside the Hall of Dinosaurs?

A Chapter 1, pages 11–14   C Chapter 3, pages 50-53, 56-59
B Chapter 2, pages 42–48   D Chapter 4, pages 79–82

UNLAWFUL TO PHOTOCOPY

PRACTICE EXERCISE

Read the following poem. Then answer the questions that follow.

HOMEWORK BY JANE YOLEN

What is it about homework
That makes me want to write
My Great Aunt Myrt to thank her for
The sweater that's too tight?

What is it about homework
That makes me pick up socks
That stink from days and days of wear,
Then clean the litter box?

What is it about homework
That makes me volunteer
To take the garbage out before
The bugs and flies appear?

What is it about homework
That makes me wash my hair
And take an hour combing out
The snags and tangles there?

What is it about homework?
You know, I wish I knew,
'Cause nights when I've got homework
I've got much too much to do!

1 If the author has homework tomorrow after school, she will most likely

A   finish it right away

B   have her friends do it for her

C   find other things to do first

D   stay home from school the next day

UNLAWFUL TO PHOTOCOPY

2 From the information in the poem, the reader can conclude that the

A   author is easily distracted   C   author is very neat
B   author has very little to do   D   author enjoys doing homework

3 Which statement best describes the author's view of homework?

A   She enjoys doing homework.
B   She believes homework is essential.
C   She prefers doing other things first.
D   She thinks homework is necessary.

4 Why does the author want to write her Great Aunt Myrt?

A   She likes the way the sweater fits.
B   Her mother asked her to write a thank you note.
C   She misses her Great Aunt Myrt.
D   She wants to avoid doing her homework.

Directions: Examine the advertisement below. Then answer the question that follows.

5 Which of the following statements from the advertisement is an opinion?

A   Mrs. Jones' old fashioned buttery popcorn is made with all natural products.
B   No other popcorn tastes as good as Mrs. Jones' popcorn clusters.
C   Mrs. Jones' Popcorn Clusters are available in three sizes.
D   Just 75 calories per serving.

UNLAWFUL TO PHOTOCOPY

CHAPTER 9

A PRACTICE SESSION 1

Before beginning this practice **Session 1**, let's review the strategies you have learned for different types of multiple-choice questions.

TEST-TAKING STRATEGIES

STEP 1: IDENTIFY THE TYPE OF READING

Before reading any passage on the test, you should:

★ Examine the title and illustrations to give you a quick idea of what the reading is about.

★ Scan through the passage to get a sense of what type of reading it is — such as a story, poem or informational article.

STEP 2: READ WITH A PURPOSE

After you have identified the type of reading selection, you should read the passage more carefully for its ideas and details. Reading with a purpose will help you to understand the passage more easily.

STORY	POETRY	INFORMATIONAL
If the passage is fiction, such as a story, novel excerpt, or play, then look for the: ❖ setting ❖ characters ❖ plot ❖ theme(s)	If the passage is a poem, and: ❖ it tells a story, look for the same things as for any story ❖ it is descriptive, determine what the poet is describing	If the passage is informational, then: ❖ determine the author's main idea, and how the factual details support this main idea

UNLAWFUL TO PHOTOCOPY

It is often a good idea to mark key parts of a passage as you read. This can help you to identify and recall the main details of a story, article or poem. Some approaches you might want to use include:

★ (Circle) main ideas.

★ Underline key words or names that may help you follow the story, such as main characters, important conflicts, or the setting.

★ Star * any words or phrases that may later help you answer questions.

For example, identify words that show a sequence or cause and effect: *as a result of, before, last, after,* etc.

★ Write comments in the margin next to the passage. For example, write "change" where a characters feelings or actions change and identify important events.

STEP 3: ANSWER THE QUESTIONS

After you read the passage, answer the questions. If you are unsure of the answer, then:

★ Start by crossing out answer choices you know are incorrect.

★ Scan the reading to find information relating to the question.

★ For questions about the <u>main idea</u>, <u>what the reading is mostly about</u>, or <u>theme</u>, consider the reading as a whole.

★ For questions about details (including <u>sequence</u>, <u>comparisons</u> or <u>cause-and-effect</u>) look for where the answer is directly stated in the passage.

★ If the answer is not stated directly, use passage details as clues to figure out the correct answer.

Unlawful to Photocopy

Read the following passage. Then answer the questions that follow.

HOW BIG MOUTH WRESTLED THE GIANT

There was once a lad known for his bragging. Everyone called him "Big Mouth." Whenever Big Mouth spoke about anything he saw, it became the biggest, or the ugliest, or the best ever. Big Mouth himself was the bravest, smartest young man in the whole country-side — according to Big Mouth.

Big Mouth was always bragging about how he would fight the giant who lived in the woods and make him cry for mercy. "I'll send him running," he said. "Wait and see!"

One day as Big Mouth went through the woods, he talked to himself. "If I meet that giant," he said, "I'll wrestle him and win."

"Halt!" cried the giant, appearing suddenly. Big Mouth took one look at the giant and jumped into the pile of trees the giant had just flung by the side of the path.

"Oh, afraid, are you?" roared the giant.

"Afraid?" cried Big Mouth. "I should say not! I'm — I'm hunting for the biggest tree to hit you with!"

The giant blinked his eyes. What kind of fellow was this? He reached in and dragged Big Mouth out by his shirttail. "Let's wrestle!" said the giant.

Struggling in the giant's grasp, Big Mouth began to sweat. His eyes bulged, and his teeth chattered with fright. "You'd better watch out!" he said.

"Watch out?" roared the giant. "Why, look at you — you're so scared, you're covered with sweat! Any minute you'll be begging for mercy!" Big Mouth wanted mercy, but his tongue just wouldn't say the word.

CONTINUED ➡

"I'm not sweating," he said. "I'm g-g-greasing myself — so you won't be able to hang on to me!" The giant almost lost him at that, for he was slippery.

"Well then," snarled the giant, tightening his grip, "why are your eyes bulging? Any minute now you'll beg me to let go so you can breathe again!"

"Oh no, I won't!" squeaked Big Mouth. "My eyes are bulging because I'm looking around for a g-g-good p-p-place to throw you!" With a bellow of rage, the giant held Big Mouth up right in front of his ugly face.

"In that case," he roared, "tell me why your teeth are chattering. Just tell me that!" With such a close view of the giant's teeth, Big Mouth nearly fainted. But not even that could stop his bragging. "M-my teeth aren't chattering!" he cried. "I'm sh-sh-sharpening them to bite off your nose!"

At hearing that, the giant clapped his hand over his nose, dropped Big Mouth to the ground, and ran away into the woods. He was never heard from again.

But in case you think this shows that bragging is a good idea, let me tell you the rest. When Big Mouth returned home, nobody believed him — not even his mother.

1 The story "How Big Mouth Wrestled the Giant" is mostly about

  A   a boy who bragged his way into and out of trouble
  B   how a boy was stronger than a giant
  C   strangers who learn to accept their differences
  D   the dangers of living in the woods

2 Big Mouth boasted that he would fight the giant because he

  A   had always hated him
  B   wanted to get revenge
  C   wanted to show he was the best
  D   thought he would win a prize

UNLAWFUL TO PHOTOCOPY

3 In the story, the giant held Big Mouth up to his face with a "bellow of rage." What does the word "bellow" mean?

A an angry roar
B a big smile
C a hungry look
D a quiet whisper

4 Why did Big Mouth say he was "greasing" himself?

A He thought the giant would let him go.
B He wanted to tell the truth.
C He thought he could slip past the giant.
D He did not want to admit he was scared.

5 What happened after Big Mouth threatened to bite the giant's nose?

A Big Mouth hid behind a tree.
B The giant bragged that he defeated Big Mouth.
C Big Mouth never bragged again.
D The giant dropped Big Mouth and ran off.

6 The next time Big Mouth tells people his story, listeners will probably

A believe him because he never lies
B ignore him since he is crazy
C not believe him because he often exaggerates
D ask him for help against other giants

7 What lesson can **best** be learned from this story?

A Giants make dangerous enemies.
B A kindness is never wasted.
C Equals make the best friends.
D Bragging can bring problems.

8 If there were another sentence at the end of the story, what would it most likely say?

A "Later, Big Mouth and the giant became life-long friends."
B "We should listen to the advice of our mother."
C "Big Mouth never returned the woods again."
D "Big Mouth gave up bragging after that."

UNLAWFUL TO PHOTOCOPY

Read the following poem and answer the questions that follow.

THE SANDPIPER

Frances Frost

At the edge of tide
He stops to wonder,
Races through
The lace of thunder.

On toothpick legs
Swift and brittle,
He runs and pipes
And his voice is little.

But small or not,
He has a notion
To outshout
The Atlantic Ocean.

9 Which of the following most fascinates the poet about sandpipers?

A   their large families

B   their bright colors

C   their protective disguises

D   their shouting at waves

10 What does the word "notion" mean in the last stanza of the poem?

A   an idea

B   a loud voice

C   a country

D   a friend

11 In the poem, the phrase "on toothpick legs" is meant to show that the legs of the sandpiper are

A   thin and delicate

B   fat and pudgy

C   wooden and hard

D   stiff and twisted

12 Which statement best describes the poet's view of sandpipers?

A   They are large but stay quiet.

B   They are fearful but pretend to be brave.

C   They are little but move quickly.

D   They are plain but think they are pretty.

UNLAWFUL TO PHOTOCOPY

Read the following selection. Then answer the questions that follow.

"YOU'RE ALIVE"

By Gail Skroback Hennessey

Mark Pfetzer shivered as he huddled from the wind raging outside his tiny tent. Weak from three exhausting weeks on Mount Everest, the 16-year-old wondered if he and the nine others on his climbing team would ever reach its 29,028-foot high top.

The violent storm out-side seemed like another hurdle after weeks of scrambling over plunging crevasses, clutching a rope for dear life as he struggled up an icy slope. Surely he could wait out the storm, he thought. What he didn't know was this storm was more than just an obstacle. When it was over, Mark would have survived the dead-liest night on Mount Everest, the world's high-est mountain.

Mount Everest

Mark caught "mountain fever" at age 12. Indoor rock-climbing and local mountains were too easy. That's when Mark decided to tackle the world's highest mountains. By 15, he had conquered mountains in Peru, Ecuador, and Argentina. Experts knew him as one of the best young climbers around.

In 1995, 15-year-old Mark was ready to attack Mount Everest. If he had succeeded, he would have been the youngest climber to do so. But at 25,000 feet, hard coughing at high altitude had caused him to break two ribs.

Mark wasted no time before planning a second attempt on Everest. He hoped to reach the top of Everest with a new group of climbers in May 1996. He discovered, however, that the mountain was just as determined not to let him succeed.

UNLAWFUL TO PHOTOCOPY

To prepare, he ran 13 miles a day, lifted weights, and ran up flights of stairs for an hour every day. But nothing could prepare him for creeping along slippery, tied-together ladders hanging across a bottomless crevasse. Or for seeing the bodies of unlucky climbers, left on the mountain because it was too dangerous to bring them down.

Then there was the altitude change. As Mark climbed higher, the air grew thinner. Every step felt like a hundred. To adjust, Mark and other climbers moved between five camps. He continued this back and forth shuttle until he was strong enough to make it to Camp Four, the last stop before the top. The journey to Camp Four was grueling.

Mark was close to what Everest climbers call the "Death Zone," about 26,000 feet up. Here, oxygen becomes scarce. Temperatures drop. Winds sear your face. "The human body doesn't accept the lack of oxygen easily at this elevation," he says.

Climbers move between camps.

Exhausted, Mark willed himself to walk five sets of 20 steps, then rest. His head pounded. In the swirl of snow, he couldn't find his feet, making deadly missteps a threat. Yet if he leaned forward to find them, he pinched the tube supplying his oxygen.

Finally, Mark stumbled into Camp Four, just ahead of a brutal, sudden storm. Winds gusted at 70 miles an hour, making the air feel a bone chilling 100 degrees below zero.

"We were safe inside the tent," Mark says. Still, his group could do nothing but wait. As the night storm wore on, Mark realized he wasn't going to reach the top of Everest. But his disappointment was nothing compared to what he felt when he heard the terrible news: Eight other climbers had died.

On the grueling climb down, Mark passed documentary filmmaker David Breashears going up to help those still stranded by the storm. Breashears congratulated Mark. When Mark replied he hadn't reached the top, Mr. Breashears just said: "You're alive."

Unlawful to Photocopy

It was then that Mark realized that maybe he hadn't reached his goal of climbing Everest — this time. But he had reached a more important one: he had survived. Now Mark is getting ready for a third Everest attempt next spring. And even if he doesn't make it this time, he'll never stop trying.

---

13 The author gives her story the title, "You're Alive," to show that

  A   Mark is a lively young man.
  B   climbing Mt. Everest requires great skill.
  C   Mark had achieved something just by surviving.
  D   Mt. Everest sometimes acts like it is a living mountain.

14 The author says that, "Mark caught 'mountain fever' at age 12." What does she mean by this sentence?

  A   Mark was deathly ill at age 12.
  B   Mark became thrilled with climbing mountains at age 12.
  C   Mark ran a fever whenever he thought of mountain climbing.
  D   Even as a young man, Mark was constantly getting sick.

15 Read this sentence from the story.

  The violent storm outside seemed like another hurdle after weeks of scrambling over plunging crevasses, clutching a rope for dear life as he struggled up an icy slope.

What does "crevasses" mean?

  A   deep cracks   C   mountains
  B   climbing equipment   D   heights

16 Which sentence from the passage describes Mt. Everest like a living being?

  A   "Clutching a rope for dear life as he struggled up an icy slope."
  B   "The human body doesn't accept the lack of oxygen easily at this elevation."
  C   "He discovered, however, that the mountain was just as determined not to let him succeed."
  D   "As the night storm wore on, Mark realized he wasn't going to reach the top of Everest."

UNLAWFUL TO PHOTOCOPY

17 Read this sentence from the article.

> He continued this back and forth shuttle until he was strong enough to make it to Camp Four, the last stop before the top.

In this sentence, the word "shuttle" means

A   travel in a motorized vehicle
B   moving close to something
C   moving between places
D   leaving alone

18 Why was Mark so determined to climb Mt. Everest?

A   His brother had climbed Mt. Everest.
B   He had already climbed other high mountains.
C   He was offered a prize to climb it.
D   His parents asked him to climb Mt. Everest.

19 Which event belongs in the empty box below?

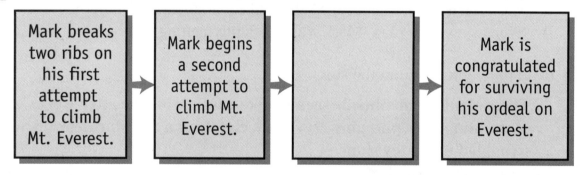

A   Mark climbs Everest a third time.
B   Mark is caught in a deadly storm.
C   Mark missteps in the "Dead Zone."
D   Mark trains by climbing stairs.

20 What conclusion can **best** be drawn from the article?

A   Mountain climbing does not pose any real dangers.
B   Experienced climbers rarely have accidents.
C   Some climbers enjoy overcoming natural challenges.
D   Mountain climbing does not require great physical ability.

21 Which information **best** shows that Mark was an experienced climber?

A   Mark took time to get his body in shape.
B   Mark liked to travel to different countries.
C   Mark was not prepared for creeping along slippery ladders.
D   Mark was unable to see his feet in the snow.

UNLAWFUL TO PHOTOCOPY

SESSION 2: LISTENING AND WRITING

Session 2 of the **Grade 4 English Language Arts Test** examines your listening and writing skills. You will be asked to listen to a passage and then to answer questions about it. You will also be asked to answer two short-response questions and one extended-response question. You will be given 45 minutes to complete Session 2. This unit will help you prepare for both parts of Session 2. You will practice listening and note-taking, and learn how to answer short-response and extended-response questions.

UNLAWFUL TO PHOTOCOPY

CHAPTER 10

LISTENING AND NOTE-TAKING

Did you know that we often learn by listening? In fact, we spend more time in school listening than reading. That is why it is so important to be a good listener. **Session 2** of the **Grade 4 English Language Arts Test** examines how skilled you are at listening.

DEVELOPING LISTENING SKILLS

Listening is more than just hearing. To *listen* means to *hear* and *understand*. Your mind has to be actively involved in listening. Focus all of your attention on the speaker. Be aware of the speaker's 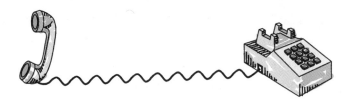 gestures, what the speaker emphasizes, and the speaker's tone and pauses. These can often help you to understand the content of what is being said.

There are many things you can do to improve your listening skills. You can:

★ listen to story tapes from the library.

★ watch a television show with the sound turned off. Study the speaker's gestures and facial expressions. Can you tell whether the topic is serious or funny? How do the speaker's gestures add meaning?

★ listen to stories read by a parent or friend. After listening, tell the speaker what you have understood about the story. Then look over what was read.

UNLAWFUL TO PHOTOCOPY

PREPARING FOR THE LISTENING TEST

During **Session 2** of the test, your teacher will read a short story to your class twice. Then you will answer some questions about this listening passage. Here are some important hints for this part of the test:

GET READY

Get ready to listen before the passage is read. Don't get distracted. Ignore any background activity or noise. Try not to let your mind wander or think about other things. Face the person who is about to read the story.

LISTEN FOR A PURPOSE

During **Session 2**, your teacher will read a story of some kind. You should concentrate on the main elements found in every story — its *setting*, *characters*, and *plot*. Here are some of the questions that you should think about as the story is being read:

★ *Where and when does the story take place?*

★ *Who are the characters? What are they like?*

★ *What is the main problem faced by the characters?*

★ *How is the problem solved?*

FOCUS ON WHAT THE SPEAKER IS SAYING

Do not focus on what the speaker looks like or the special sound of that person's voice. Instead, concentrate on what the reader is *saying*.

Look at the reader, except when you are taking notes or picturing the story in your mind. Pay special attention to any gestures (*movements*) or changes in voice that the reader uses in telling the story. Listen to pauses that give emphasis to some sentences. These are all clues that can help you better understand the story.

UNLAWFUL TO PHOTOCOPY

BE AN ACTIVE LISTENER

Just as a good reader is active, so is a good listener. In your mind, you should picture what is going on in the listening passage as it is read. Make predictions and see if they happen in the story. Ask questions to yourself. See if they are answered as you listen to more of the story.

★ **The First Reading.** The first time you hear the story, listen for the "big" picture. Try to get an idea of the story's overall meaning. Make a mental picture of the characters and imagine what they are doing.

★ **The Second Reading.** The second time you listen, focus more on particular details. Listen carefully to any words or sentences you did not understand the first time the story was read. Make sure you know the characters, setting and plot. Also, try to answer any questions you may still have about what happens in the story.

DEVELOPING NOTE-TAKING SKILLS

As you listen to the story, you are encouraged to take notes. Note-taking will help you to keep track of the story and focus on what the speaker is reading.

The reader will speak faster than you will be able to write. Do not try to write your notes in complete sentences. That will take too much time. Instead, keep your notes short and brief. Use abbreviations and key words as reminders.

Forms of Note-taking. You will not have time to write down everything the reader says. Instead you must choose carefully what you write down in your notes. One way of taking notes is shown on the following page. Fill in the information on this form as you listen to the story. In the final lines marked "Other Information," write down the theme, conclusion or any other information from the story that you think is important.

UNLAWFUL TO PHOTOCOPY

Setting: _____

Main Characters:

★ _____

★ _____

★ _____

Problem(s) Faced By Main Character(s) _____
_____

Main Story Events

★ _____
_____

★ _____
_____

★ _____
_____

Other Information: _____
_____
_____

UNLAWFUL TO PHOTOCOPY

Remember not to write down too much while the story is being read. Just jot down a few words for your notes so that you can concentrate on listening to the story. Concentrate on the *who*, *what*, *when*, *where*, *how* and *why*. After the second reading is finished, you can complete your notes.

COMMON NOTE-TAKING ABBREVIATIONS

Here are some common abbreviations. You can develop your own abbreviations as you become more comfortable at note-taking.

+	=	and
St.	=	street
Bc	=	because

K	=	Katie (use the first letter for a name)
2	=	to
P	=	problem

For example, suppose you listened to a story in which the main problem was a girl named Katy and her Mom get lost while shopping. This can be shown in note-taking form as:

$$P = K + \text{Mom lost shopping}$$

PRACTICE EXERCISE

Listening and note-taking are skills that require lots of practice. Practice listening to stories and taking notes while someone else is reading. Ask a teacher, parent, or friend to read aloud twice "The Son and the Thief" on page 196. Use the note-taking form provided on the previous page or a separate sheet of paper to record your notes.

DURING THE FIRST READING

The first time the passage is read, try to get an overall idea of what it is about. Take a few notes if you wish. Practice using the techniques for listening and note-taking that you just learned.

DURING THE SECOND READING

The second time the passage is read, continue filling out the note-taking form. Complete the form after the reading is over. When you are finished with your note-taking, ask yourself:

 Did I record the main elements of the story correctly?

 Is there anything important that I left out?

After you are satisfied with your notes, compare them with the form found on page 196.

UNLAWFUL TO PHOTOCOPY

CHAPTER 11

SHORT-RESPONSE QUESTIONS

Unlike multiple-choice questions, short-response questions will ask you to do more than just select the right answer. A short-response question requires you to provide the correct answer yourself. In **Session 2**, two questions will require you to write short responses based on the listening passage. This chapter will examine the various ways these questions might be asked and show you how to write your answer.

WRITING A SHORT-RESPONSE ANSWER

Short-response questions usually focus on your basic understanding of the story. Some questions will ask you to complete the answer in a graphic organizer. Almost always, the answer will be stated directly in the listening passage. This means the answer will be spoken when the story is read aloud. Often, the question will ask you to provide specific details from the story. Therefore, you must pay careful attention to what the reader says.

You should base your written answer on the information in the story. To write your response, you will have to remember details from the story. Or, you may find the answer by checking your notes. After you have completed your response, you should look back at the question. Ask yourself whether you have answered the question with the specific information required from the story.

QUESTION WORDS PROVIDE THE KEY TO THE TASK

Most short-response questions will ask you about the *what*, *how*, or *why* of the story. The question words themselves — *what*, *how*, and *why* — provide the keys to what you are expected to do.

UNLAWFUL TO PHOTOCOPY

Let's begin by looking more closely at short-response questions that use *what*, *how*, and *why* based on the story "The Son and the Thief" that you listened to in the practice exercise in the last chapter.

"WHAT" QUESTIONS

What questions will usually ask you to *identify* or *explain* specific things in a story. For example, this type of question might ask you to identify the setting, characters, or main events of the story.

What questions about details can be phrased in a variety of ways. For example, the following question could be asked about the story, "The Son and the Thief":

What did Li ask the thief to leave behind?

To answer this question, you have to recall specifically what Li told the thief. He asked the thief to leave behind an old pot that he used to cook his mother's meals. If the thief took the pot, Li said he would be unable to cook for his mother.

A *what question* may sometimes ask you to go beyond what is directly stated in the story. You might be asked to draw a conclusion, to make a prediction, or to state a lesson that can be learned from the story. Frequently, such questions will ask you to provide one or more details from the story to support your answer.

CHECKING YOUR UNDERSTANDING

What important lesson does the thief learn from Li?
Provide details from the story to support your answer.

_____

_____

The next page describes some strategies you can use to answer a *what question*.

UNLAWFUL TO PHOTOCOPY

UNLOCKING THE ANSWER

First, look to see *what* the question asks for.
★ Does the question ask for a **detail** that was stated directly in the story?
★ Does the question ask for a lesson or conclusion?

Next, try to recall the story detail the question asks for.
★ If you cannot remember, look over your notes. These may remind you of the detail.
★ If the question asks for a **lesson** or **conclusion**, think about what you can conclude from what happens in the story. Review page 87 on drawing conclusions.

Finally, write your answer. Sometimes you will only need to write a few words to complete a graphic organizer.

Now you try answering a *what question*:

CHECKING YOUR UNDERSTANDING

What things did the thief try to steal from Li and his mother?

_____

_____

"HOW" QUESTIONS

How simply means "in what way." A *how question* might ask you to tell the way in which something in the story is done: *How does Li take care of his mother?*

UNLAWFUL TO PHOTOCOPY

A *how question* might also ask about the way in which a character in the story changes. Here is another example of a *how question*:

CHECKING YOUR UNDERSTANDING

How has the thief changed by the end of the story?

_____

_____

To answer this question, you have to think about what the thief is like when he breaks into Li's house. He has entered Li's home for a specific reason — to steal objects of value from both Li and his mother. Remember that the thief makes Li and his mother sit in the corner while he searches through their house looking for things to steal. Compare this image of the thief with how the thief has changed by the end of the story. Think about what the thief does and says after he learns of Li's modesty and devotion to his mother.

A *how question* may also ask you to compare story details. You could be asked to describe how two characters or events in the story are different or alike. For example, you might be asked the following:

CHECKING YOUR UNDERSTANDING

How were the thief and Li different?
Provide details from the story to support your answer.

_____

_____

_____

The next page has some hints to make it easier to answer a *how question*.

UNLAWFUL TO PHOTOCOPY

UNLOCKING THE ANSWER

The question word *how* often relates to a series of actions or events. In this case, your task is to show the ways these actions or events are connected. Describe each event and show the way these events fit together to explain the whole.

To show *how* a character changes, describe that character at the start of the story. Then describe this character later in the story after he or she is changed by what happens.

If asked to show *how* two characters are **alike** or **different**:
★ To show how two characters are *alike*, point out their similarities. For example, both Li and the thief live in China. Neither is rich. Both are struggling to survive.
★ To show how two characters are *different*, identify what is true of each one but **not** of both of them. For example, Li is extremely honest and devoted to his mother. The thief is dishonest and lives by stealing.

Now you try answering a *how question*:

CHECKING YOUR UNDERSTANDING

How did Li react when the thief tried to steal the old pot? Provide details from the story to support your answer.

UNLAWFUL TO PHOTOCOPY

"WHY" QUESTIONS

Why questions focus on causes. They ask you to give one or more reasons *why* something took place.

Often a *why question* asks you to tell about the motives or reasons that led a character to do something. Try answering the following *why question*:

CHECKING YOUR UNDERSTANDING

Why did the thief leave Li's house with an empty bag?

_____

_____

To answer this question, think about why the thief decides to empty his bag of objects he has taken. What did Li say to the thief to bring about this change of heart? How did Li's comment make the thief feel about what he was doing?

When answering *why questions*, you should apply the following steps:

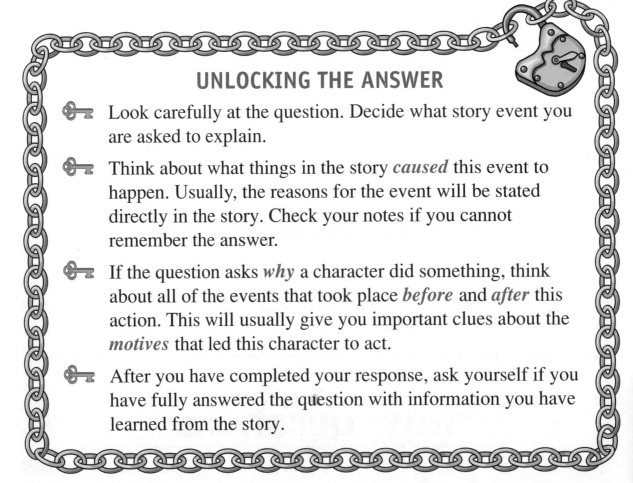

UNLOCKING THE ANSWER

- Look carefully at the question. Decide what story event you are asked to explain.

- Think about what things in the story **caused** this event to happen. Usually, the reasons for the event will be stated directly in the story. Check your notes if you cannot remember the answer.

- If the question asks **why** a character did something, think about all of the events that took place **before** and **after** this action. This will usually give you important clues about the *motives* that led this character to act.

- After you have completed your response, ask yourself if you have fully answered the question with information you have learned from the story.

UNLAWFUL TO PHOTOCOPY

Let's see how well you can apply these steps to answering a *why question*:

CHECKING YOUR UNDERSTANDING

Why did Li speak up to the thief?

_____

_____

_____

COMPLETING GRAPHIC ORGANIZERS

A **graphic organizer** presents information in boxes, circles or some other visual form. Some short-response questions will ask you to fill in these shapes with details from the story. For example, you might be asked to complete:

| A web or concept map | A timeline or sequence map | A Venn diagram |

Usually, you will only have to write a few names or words in the empty spaces. These questions generally do not ask you to write complete sentences. Let's take a closer look at *graphic-organizer questions*:

WEB OR CONCEPT MAPS

A **web** or **concept map** places a topic from the reading (*such as a concept, character or event*) in the center of the organizer. This topic is then surrounded with supporting examples, facts or details. This type of graphic organizer is often used to describe an idea, character, place or event. It can help you to see easily the details that make up that person, thing or idea. Complete the concept map on the next page by answering the following *what question* based on "The Son and the Thief":

What are four of the things that Li and his mother owned?
Write your answer in the empty ovals of the web.

UNLAWFUL TO PHOTOCOPY

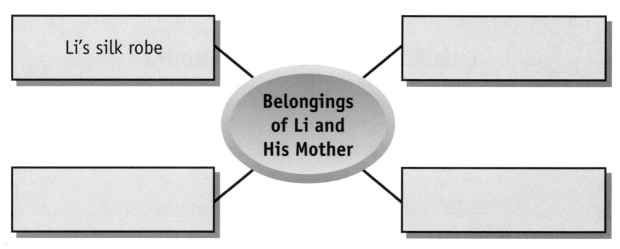

Notice how the web map is completed by listing the objects owned by Li and his mother. One of these is Li's silk robe. What three other objects are mentioned?

TIMELINE OR SEQUENCE MAP

As you know, the plot of a story consists of a series of events. A *sequence map* or *timeline* traces how these events have developed over time. This type of graphic organizer presents events in the order in which they occurred. A question about a timeline will ask you to fill in a missing event or detail.

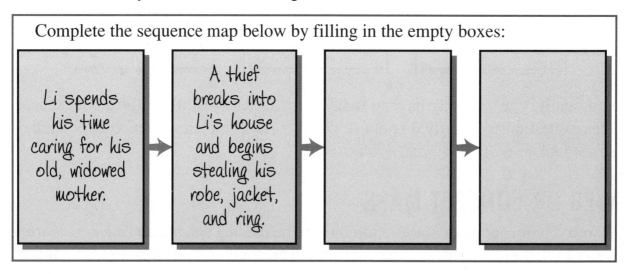

Complete the sequence map below by filling in the empty boxes:

VENN DIAGRAMS

A **Venn diagram** is a useful way to show information when you wish to compare or contrast something. It uses overlapping circles or other shapes to show how two or more items are the same or different. Whatever is unique to each item or topic is placed in the part of the oval that does not overlap. Think of completing a Venn diagram as a special type of *compare-and-contrast* or *how question*.

UNLAWFUL TO PHOTOCOPY

Try answering the following question:

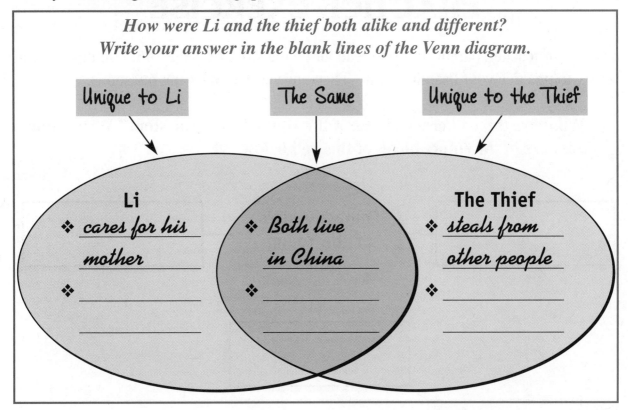

How were Li and the thief both alike and different?
Write your answer in the blank lines of the Venn diagram.

Unique to Li   The Same   Unique to the Thief

Li
❖ *cares for his mother*
❖ _____

❖ *Both live in China*
❖ _____

The Thief
❖ *steals from other people*
❖ _____

To help you answer this question, look at the hints in the *Unlocking the Answer* box on page 119. This box provides ideas on how Li and the thief were both alike and different.

HOW YOUR ANSWERS WILL BE SCORED

Your short-response answers will be scored together with your extended-response answers as part of a "cluster." In order to get the highest score, be sure to provide the specific information that each question asks for. This means you need to include details and examples to support your ideas. The information that you provide must be based on the story. If you include anything beyond what is in the story in your answer, it must be directly linked to the task.

★ If your answers include some correct information but are too general, incomplete, or partly incorrect, they will not receive full credit.

★ If your answers are completely inaccurate, confused or do not relate to the questions, they will receive no credit at all.

UNLAWFUL TO PHOTOCOPY

PRACTICE EXERCISE

Have your teacher, parent or friend read aloud the story on page 195. Use this story as a way to practice your listening skills. Then answer the following questions:

1   What are three characteristics of the young boy in the story? Write your answers in the empty boxes of the web below.

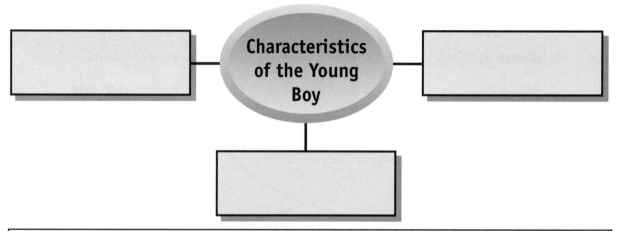

2   Why did the boy refuse to take twigs from the royal forest? Use details from the story to support your answer.

_____

_____

_____

_____

3   In the chart below, write how the emperor feels about each of the following:

	The Emperor's Feelings
His people	
The boy's honesty	

UNLAWFUL TO PHOTOCOPY

CHAPTER 12

ANSWERING EXTENDED-RESPONSE QUESTIONS

In addition to asking you to complete short-response questions, **Session 2** will require you to answer one extended-response question. The answer to this type of question should be one or more paragraphs. An extended-response question will always require a complete written answer.

Here is an example of an extended-response question based on the story you listened to in the last chapter, "The Emperor and the Boy":

> **How are the emperor and the boy different and alike?**
> **Use details from the story to support your answer.**

Unlike a short-response answer, your extended-response answer will receive two separate scores:

★ **Response to the Question:** Your extended-response will be scored with your short answers as part of a "cluster." Your score will be based on how well you answer the question and support your answer with details from the listening passage.

★ **Writing Conventions:** You will receive a second score for how well your answer follows standard writing conventions: capitalization, punctuation, spelling, and usage.

MODEL ANSWERS

Sometimes it helps to read other student responses to see how they have answered the same extended-response question. The question above was given to a class of fourth-grade students. You can read some their responses on the next page.

Unlawful to Photocopy

After you read each student's response, give it a score from 0 to 4.

★ **No Points.** A score of "0" is the lowest score. It basically means the student has not answered the question at all. A score of no points means the response is either incorrect, unrelated to the question, or hard to understand.

★ **Four Points.** A score of 4 is the highest score. Give this score if it means the student has completely answered the question. A score of "4" points means the response is well supported with details and examples from the listening passage. Moreover, the student has organized and expressed these ideas and details well.

On the actual test, your extended-response answer for Session 2 will be scored along with your two short responses as one complete cluster. Together, these three answers will receive a score of 0 to 4 points. Your score will be based on how well you understand the passage and answer the three questions.

Now read the following three responses. After you have completed reading each answer, give it a score and explain why you gave it that score.

STUDENT RESPONSE A:

The emperor and the boy are alike and different. They both are very caring people. The emperor cares about his subjects. He goes in disguise so he can discover what his subjects really think. The boy cares about his family. He goes around picking up twigs for their fire. The emperor, however, is rich and powerful. He makes the laws for his people. The boy is poor and obeys these laws. His family does not even have enough wood for a good fire.

EXPLAINING YOUR SCORE

Your score? _____ Explain why you gave that score. _____

_____

_____

UNLAWFUL TO PHOTOCOPY

STUDENT RESPONSE B:

The emperor and the boy are alike and different. The emperor is an all-powerful ruler. As ruler over his subjects, he makes laws that they must obey. For example, he has ruled that no one can use wood collected from the floor of the royal forest. Anyone who enters the royal forest to collect this wood breaks the law and will be punished. The boy is collecting twigs and sticks to make a fire for his family. He does not go into the royal forest. He thinks the emperor's law is unjust. Even though he does not like this law, the boy refuses to disobey it.

EXPLAINING YOUR SCORE

Your score? _____ Explain why you gave that score. _____

_____

_____

STUDENT RESPONSE C:

The emperor is better off than the boy. He is powerfull and rich He makes laws for the land. He has money to give to the boyz family. The boy is poor, his family does not have wood for a good fire.

EXPLAINING YOUR SCORE

Your score? _____ Explain why you gave that score. _____

_____

_____

UNLAWFUL TO PHOTOCOPY

THE ELEMENTS OF GOOD WRITING

On the actual test, an extended response will be given a score based on five characteristics:

FOCUS:
How well you stick to the topic and answer the question

ORGANIZATION:
How clearly you organize your answer

DEVELOPMENT:
How well you support your ideas with details

STYLE:
How well you express yourself

MECHANICS:
How well you follow the rules of capitalization, spelling, punctuation and usage

Think of these five characteristics — *focus*, *organization*, *development*, *style*, and *mechanics* — as the **elements** of good writing.

FOCUS

Focus refers to how well you keep your writing focused on your topic. This means you should clearly identify the topic you are writing about at the beginning of your response and then stick to it.

Think of your topic as an imaginary umbrella that covers the rest of your response. It provides a unifying theme that helps bring the different parts of your answer together into a whole. Everything you write should directly relate in some way to that topic.

When you write an extended response in the **Grade 4 English Language Arts Test**, the question actually provides your focus.

UNLAWFUL TO PHOTOCOPY

Be sure your response answers the question:

★ **What.** If the question asks *what*, make sure your answer identifies and describes *what* the question asks for.

★ **How.** If the question asks *how*, make sure your answer explains or describes *how* something happens, *how* two things are alike or different, or *how* a character changes. In the sample question on page 125, students had to describe *how* the two characters were alike and different.

★ **Why.** If the question asks *why*, make sure you give the reasons *why* the event you are trying to explain happened.

★ **Give Your Opinion.** Some extended-response questions may ask you to give your opinion or evaluate something. For example, the question might ask: In your opinion, would you consider the emperor to be a good ruler? To answer this kind of question, give your opinion and the reason behind it. Be sure to use details and examples from the listening passage to support your reasons.

When you answer an extended-response question, make sure your ideas and details clearly relate to the focus of your task. When you read over your work, cross out any ideas or details that do not help you to answer the question. Now let's look at the student responses you just scored.

Response A has a clear focus. The first sentence echoes the question. To echo the question, you simply repeat it as a statement. This sets the focus for the paragraph. In this case the first sentence explains what the paragraph will discuss — how the two characters are alike and different. Everything else the student wrote stayed within this focus, and there are many supporting details.

Response B lacks a clear focus. The response begins well by providing a first sentence that echoes the question. However, the rest of the paragraph fails to show how the emperor and the boy are alike or different. Instead, the response gives details about the emperor's powers and what the boy does. Response B never really tells the reader how the two characters are alike and different. Although this answer is the longest of the responses, it does not answer the question. It is more important to provide the correct information needed to answer the question than it is to write a long answer.

Response C is incomplete. It gives differences between the emperor and the poor boy, but it fails to provide any similarities.

UNLAWFUL TO PHOTOCOPY

ORGANIZATION

Organization refers to how well you bring your ideas and details together. Good writing has to be organized in a logical and orderly way. If not, the reader will become confused. A good extended response is usually organized into three parts:

★ **The Introduction.** The introduction tells your reader what your response will be about. It provides the focus of your answer. Often, you can simply echo the question. Two of the student responses you just read began by echoing the question.

★ **The Body.** The body is the main part of your answer. It gives your main ideas along with supporting details. You should be sure to provide specific information — examples and details from the passage — in your answer. The details in your essay should be organized in some logical way. You may want to present these details in the order in which they happened, or in their order of importance.

★ **The Conclusion.** If you write several paragraphs, you should end your response with a conclusion. The conclusion signals to the reader that your writing has come to an end. It often summarizes your main ideas. If your response is short, such as a single paragraph, you may not need to provide a conclusion.

Transitions. To make your ideas and supporting details clearer to the reader, you should use transition words and phrases. Some of the most common transitions include *afterwards*, *meanwhile*, *next*, *however*, *in addition*, *then*, and *therefore*. Transitions act as signposts to show the reader that you are moving from one point to another. They show relationships between ideas or details. You can learn more about transitions in the *Appendix* at the back of this book.

UNLAWFUL TO PHOTOCOPY

Response A is well organized. It begins by echoing the question. It then tells one way the two characters are alike. Next, the response explains two ways in which the characters are different.

Response B is not well organized. The student begins by echoing the question, but then wanders off to describe the emperor and the boy. The response never identifies the similarities and differences between them.

Response C has a clear plan of organization but is incomplete. There is no introduction. The details show how the emperor and the boy differ, but not how they are alike. There are spelling errors and a run-on sentence.

DEVELOPMENT OF IDEAS

Good writers use details and examples to explain and clarify their ideas.

A good extended response gives examples and details from the listening passage to illustrate its main points. These details tell about the *who*, *what*, *when*, *where*, *how* and *why* of what the writer is describing or explaining. Be as specific as you can. The reader should be able to picture in his or her own mind the same thoughts that the writer is trying to express.

*A good writer is able to write down thoughts
in a way that the reader can picture the same thoughts.
Clear and precise details help in this process.*

UNLAWFUL TO PHOTOCOPY

Now look again at the three responses at the beginning of this chapter. How well are they supported with details from the listening passage?

Response A states that both the emperor and the boy are caring. The response then uses story details to support this statement. The emperor cares about his subjects, so he uses a disguise to learn their true opinions. The boy cares about his family, so he helps them by gathering twigs.

Next, the response states the emperor is all-powerful. The student then supports this statement with another detail from the story — the emperor makes the laws for his subjects. This response is therefore well supported: it uses details from the listening passage to support each of its general statements.

How well do the other two student responses support their answers with details from the story?

Response B _____

_____

Response C _____

_____

WRITING STYLE

Not everyone wears the same style of blue jeans. People wear different styles to express themselves. Just as with clothing, there are different styles in writing.

You can show your originality and creativity by the way in which you decide to present your ideas. To develop your own writing style, think about your reader and the impression you want to make on him or her. Part of the impression you make will depend on your choice of words and sentence patterns.

UNLAWFUL TO PHOTOCOPY

Word Choice. Interesting words get the reader involved in your response. They help the reader to form a mental picture of what you are writing about. The right words can help readers to *see*, *hear*, *taste*, *smell* or *feel* what you are writing about.

In your response, choose precise and descriptive words. Avoid vague language by using specific, descriptive words. For example, "splintered" is a more precise word than "broken" because it tells readers that something has broken into many tiny pieces — too many to ever be repaired. A "shiny, red Ford van" is more precise and descriptive than simply writing a "car." This choice of words makes it easier for the reader to picture what is going on.

★ **Sentence Patterns.** Just as good writers consider their choice of words carefully, they also vary their sentence patterns. Look in the *Appendix* at the back of this book for some sentence patterns you might use.

Which of the sample student responses earlier in this chapter was the most interesting to read? Which of the responses had sentences with their own unique style and flavor? Which responses were the most clearly expressed?

Response A is well written. It uses interesting and varied words, such as "caring," "subjects," "disguise," "discover," and "twigs," The author uses transition words such as "however."

Response B is not well organized or focused. But it does have an interesting style. The author uses transitions, such as "for example," has an interesting vocabulary and employs a variety of sentence types.

Response C is not well written. It lacks transitions, and contains spelling errors. The author's sentences are simple and the choice of words is limited.

WRITING MECHANICS

Writing mechanics refers to how well your writing follows the rules of standard written English — *spelling*, *capitalization*, *punctuation*, and *usage*. Your extended response will receive a separate score for writing mechanics.

UNLAWFUL TO PHOTOCOPY

Some important rules you should follow in writing your response can be found in the *Appendix* of this book.

Now that you have looked at *focus*, *organization*, *development*, *style*, and *mechanics*, what score do you think each of the three responses should receive? **Response A** has a clear focus, and completely answers the question. It is well organized and supports the points it makes with details from the story. It uses interesting words and sentence patterns, without mistakes in mechanics. It is clearly the best of the three student responses.

THE WRITING PROCESS

Now that you are familiar with the ingredients of a good answer, how do you put them all together? In this section, you will learn the four steps for drafting an answer to an extended-response question. These are sometimes known as the **steps of the writing process**:

Analyze the question	**Plan your answer**	**Write your answer**	**Revise your answer**

STEP 1: ANALYZE THE QUESTION

The first step in answering an extended-response question is to read the question carefully. Like a short-response question, it will ask about the listening passage.

Examine the "Question" Word. Every short answer or extended-response question will include a "question" word. Recall the "question" words that you learned about in the last chapter — *what*, *how*, or *why*. Extended-response questions may also ask you to give your opinion about something and to explain or defend it.

UNLAWFUL TO PHOTOCOPY

The key to writing your answer is to do what the "question" word asks you to do. Remember, this question word should provide the *focus* of your answer. For example, the model question might ask you to compare two characters: "*How* are the emperor and the boy alike and different?" Then you know you have to give similarities and differences.

An extended-response question might also ask you to *explain what* lesson can be learned from the story. Or it could ask *what* the title of the story means, or *how* a character has changed in the story. In each case, the question word tells you what you have to do.

If you have to give your opinion, such as whether the emperor was a good ruler or not, you should list the reasons why he was a good ruler or bad ruler. Then decide your opinion and find supporting details to defend it.

STEP 2: PLAN YOUR ANSWER

After you analyze the question, you should plan your answer. You should look over your notes to review what you have just heard and to develop your own ideas to answer the question. For example, to answer how the emperor and the boy were *alike*, you have to think about each character and how they were similar.

You might recall that the boy helped his family by gathering sticks. He was very honest and refused to break the law by taking wood from the royal forest.

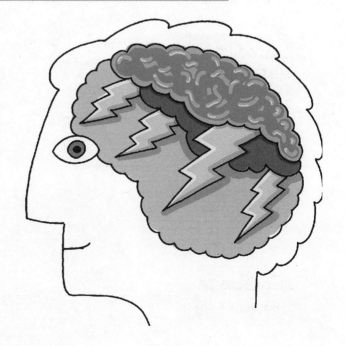

UNLAWFUL TO PHOTOCOPY

You should also recall that the emperor was rich and powerful, but cared deeply about the people he ruled. He disguised himself so that he could see the true conditions in which they lived. Later, he rewarded the boy for his honesty, and changed the unjust law about the royal forests.

Just remembering all these details is *not* enough. You have to *use* these story details to answer the question. You need to describe which details and ideas show how the emperor and the boy were alike. Both characters are caring people. Both characters respect the law, and both appear to be honest. The emperor and the boy share these characteristics even though their lives are very different.

Now you are ready to organize your ideas and story details for your written response. There are many ways to organize your answer. For example, you might just make a list of similarities and differences. Or you can make an outline or a web. Many students organize their answer in the form of a **"hamburger:"** The top bun is the *introduction*, the patties of meat form the *body* of the answer, and the bottom bun is the *conclusion*.

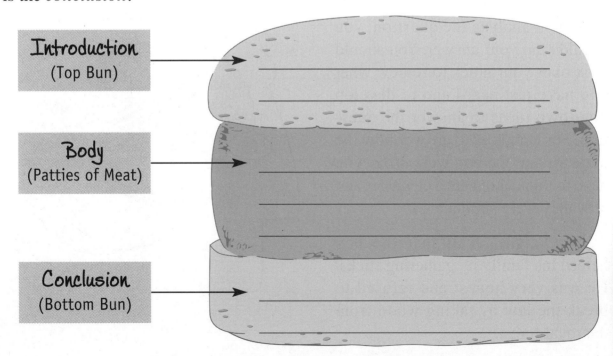

UNLAWFUL TO PHOTOCOPY

★ The *introduction* tells the reader what you are writing about. It provides the focus for your answer. Often, it can echo the question.

★ The *body* of your answer is where you put your main ideas and supporting details. Remember, it is important to use specific evidence from the listening passage to support your ideas.

★ The *conclusion* often summarizes your main idea and tells the reader that your answer has come to an end.

For example, you might conclude an extended response answer by writing, "Therefore, we can see that the emperor and the boy were both alike and different in many ways."

STEP 3: WRITING YOUR ANSWER

Now you are ready to write your answer. Turn each point of your plan into one or more complete sentences. Your first sentence can often *echo* the question by turning it into a statement. Then give your main points and supporting details. Finally, you can return to your opening idea in your conclusion.

Be aware of your writing style. Choose precise words, vary your sentence patterns and follow the rules of good writing mechanics.

STEP 4: REVISE YOUR ANSWER

In the final step of the writing process, you should reread your response and correct it. Read your response silently to yourself. Pretend you are someone else, reading the draft for the very first time. Make sure you have answered the question and provided examples and details from the passage to support your main idea.

Remember that you will receive a second grade based on your ability to follow the rules of standard written English. As you read your work, be sure to look for writing errors.

UNLAWFUL TO PHOTOCOPY

Pay close attention to *capitalization*, *punctuation*, *spelling* and *usage*. Make sure every sentence begins with a capital letter and ends with a period, question mark, or exclamation point. If you find something that needs to be changed, either erase it or cross it out neatly. Write insertions above the line, using a "caret" mark (∧) to show where they go.

PRACTICE EXERCISE

Now you try it. Answer the following extended-response questions based on the story: "The Emperor and the Boy."

> **How does the emperor change from the beginning of the story to the end? Use details from the story to support your answer.**

Use the graphic organizer below to plan your answer:

Ways in which the Emperor Changes   **Supporting Details**

Emperor at beginning: _____

_____

_____

_____

_____

_____

_____

Emperor at end: _____

_____

_____

_____

_____

_____

_____

UNLAWFUL TO PHOTOCOPY

Use the space below to write your response:

UNLAWFUL TO PHOTOCOPY

Now let's try answering a second extended-response question based on the story: "The Emperor and the Boy.'

> **What is your opinion of the emperor? Do you consider him to be a good ruler? Use details from the story to support your answer.**

Use the space below to write your response:

CHAPTER 13

SESSION 2: A PRACTICE LISTENING PASSAGE

In the last few chapters, you learned how to listen, take notes, and answer short-response and extended-response questions. In this chapter, you will practice your new skills by listening to a story just like those on the real test. The story is called **"The Chest of Broken Glass."** The story is found in the *Teacher's Guide and Answer Key* accompanying this book.

Your teacher will read the story **twice**. As you listen, you may use the space below to take notes. You can create an outline, web, or any other form of notes you feel comfortable making. You may use these notes to answer the questions that follow. Your notes on this page will **NOT** count toward your final score.

NOTES

UNLAWFUL TO PHOTOCOPY

Based on the listening passage, answer the following three questions:

1 Why do the three sons decide to guard their father's chest? Use details from the story to support your answer.

2 In the boxes below, write how each son reacts when he learns that the chest is full of broken glass.

Oldest son ——→

Middle son ——→

Youngest son ——→

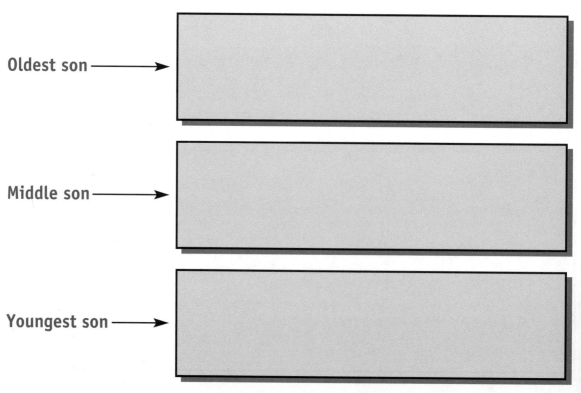

UNLAWFUL TO PHOTOCOPY

3 Do you think the father was right to leave his sons a chest of broken glass? Use details from the story to support your answer.

You may plan your answer in the box below if you wish. Do not write your final answer here. This box is for you to write your first draft.

Now, use a separate sheet of paper to write your final answer.

Unlawful to Photocopy

SESSION 3:
READING AND WRITING

📖 **Chapter 14:** Questions on Paired Readings

📖 **Chapter 15:** Session 3: Practice Answering Linked Passages

In **Session 3**, you will read two passages that are related in some way. Then you will be asked to answer three short-response and one extended-response question.

In Chapter 14, you will learn how to approach paired readings. This is followed by a complete practice **Session 3** in Chapter 15.

You already know how to answer both short-response and extended-response questions from **Session 2**. In **Session 3**, you will have the ability to look over the passages to help you write your answers. Some of the questions will ask you to make connections between both reading passages.

UNLAWFUL TO PHOTOCOPY

CHAPTER 14

QUESTIONS ON PAIRED READINGS

As you know, in **Session 3** you will be asked to read two passages. These passages will be *related* or *linked* in some way. One of these passages will be a literary text, such as a story or poem. The second passage will be an informational reading.

After reading the passages, you will be asked to answer **three** short-response questions and **one** extended-response question. Some or all of the short-response questions will focus on one of the two readings. The extended-response question will usually ask something about *both* readings.

In this chapter, you will learn how to answer questions based on paired readings.

READING LINKED PASSAGES

The reading passages in **Session 3** will be *related* or *linked* in some way:

★ **Topic.** The two passages may deal with the same *topic*. Information in one reading may help to explain what happens in the other reading. For example, both passages might examine the challenges of living in a big city. The first passage could be a report about problems faced by American cities. The second could be a story about a boy living in an apartment building in Brooklyn, New York.

★ **Theme.** The two passages may deal with the same *theme*. For example, they could both focus on feelings of anger or acts of courage.

UNLAWFUL TO PHOTOCOPY

As you read the two passages, remember to use the seven strategies of good readers:

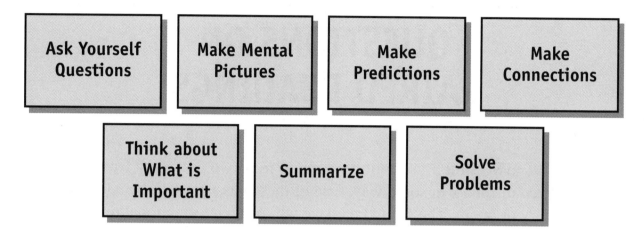

You should also ask yourself the following special questions when reading linked passages:

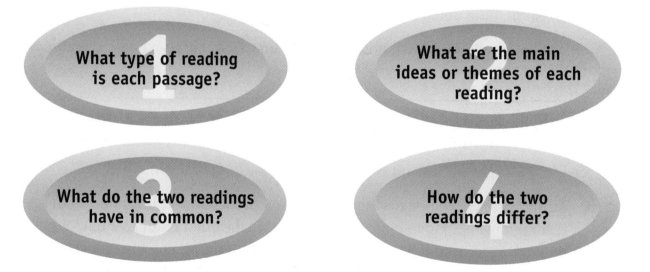

Sometimes it may help to make a Venn diagram of the two readings:

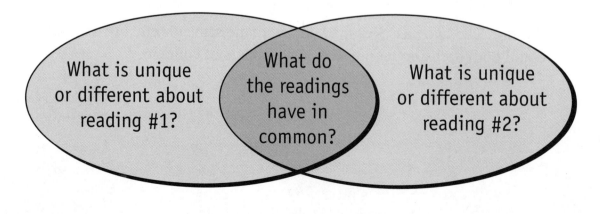

UNLAWFUL TO PHOTOCOPY

SAMPLE LINKED PASSAGES

Now that you know how to approach linked passages, read the following two selections. These passages are similar to those you might find on the actual test.

KILLER *by Sandy Fox*

Killer, they called him. He stood in the field, head down, bony ribs showing. As I walked past on my way home from school, I stopped whistling. "Hey, Champion!" I called.

He wiggled an ear and turned his head. This was progress. Last year, he'd run everytime I walked by.

Dad said he'd killed Old Man Wiggins's son. The scar on his gray flank was where Old Man Wiggins tried to kill him. The horse had raced off into the woods, and Dad said the old man had yelled after him, "Go starve to death, then!"

That must have been ten years ago, and Killer — mangy, bony, with matted mane and tail — was still alive. I didn't call him Killer. Dad said you call someone what you want him to be. To me he was Champion. I pulled out some carrots. "Champion! Come get your carrots."

His neck bent toward me, and I heard him exhale.[1] "Come on. I won't hurt you." He didn't take a single step in my direction. I sighed. He'd been coming closer to the fence each afternoon, and I'd thought I was getting somewhere. I put the carrots inside the fence and walked off, whistling "When the Saints Go Marching In."

---

[1]breathe out

UNLAWFUL TO PHOTOCOPY

CONTINUED →

When I was little and scared, Dad taught me to whistle. I'd gotten into the habit of whistling whenever I walked by the trees and the rusted car bodies next to Champion's field. I wasn't scared or anything. Whistling relaxed me.

The next afternoon I passed by Champion's field again. The carrots lay uneaten by the fence. "What's the matter, Champ?" His ears flickered and his head swung around. His tail stuck out from his body, and he snorted. When he lifted his back foot, I saw a barbed wire wrapped around it.

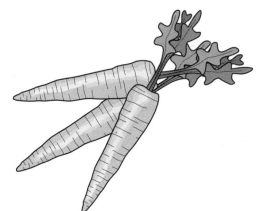

He'd been standing there all night and all day. Without food or water, he'd die. Dad wouldn't be home for hours, and Old Man Wiggins would shoot him as soon as look at him. Would Champ let me help him or was he really a mean killer?

His big brown eyes looked at me again. I wiggled through the fence. Champ tried to back up but then stood still, his ears pinned back. I swallowed, licked my lips, and began to whistle. "O when the saints, O when the saints …"

Champ's ears flipped forward, and he nickered. I whistled to drown out the pounding of my heart as I walked up to him. He flinched when I touched him. His eyes rolled.

"It's O.K. I won't hurt you." Carefully I slid my hand down his side. I could feel him trembling. He's as scared as I am, I thought.

CONTINUED

UNLAWFUL TO PHOTOCOPY

I began to whistle again as I slowly slid my hand to his backside. The barbed wire dug into his leg and around his thigh. I'd have to hurt him to set him free. I'd have to bend close to his sharp hoofs and lean under him.

I looked at him and saw him looking at me. "Will you stand still for this?" I asked him. "I'm sorry, but it's going to hurt." He bobbed his head. "Good." I smiled. Grabbing the rusted wire, I tried to thread it between his back legs. He cow-kicked and I froze. If he went crazy, we could both be killed.

Automatically, I began whistling under my breath. He put his hind leg down. I waited a minute until his muscles relaxed and he let out a breath. Slowly I bent over and unwound another twist. Gently I tugged it loose. Champ flinched but stood quietly as the barb pulled off matted hair and skin.

"I'm sorry, Champ. I'm trying to be gentle." Blood oozed from the cut, soaking into the ground. I pulled more wire from his skin, unwinding the rusted mass around the tree that had anchored the wire.

Now that he was free, would he run, kick or bite? Champ kept his eyes on me. I froze as he walked toward me. He blew gently in my face and sniffed my chest.

Slowly my hand touched his cheek. He stiffened and then relaxed. "You are a champion!" I grinned. As I walked back to the fence, Champ walked beside me — limping, but walking.

UNLAWFUL TO PHOTOCOPY

HOW HORSES COMMUNICATE

By Dorothy Hinshaw Patent

Horses use sound to communicate messages to one another. Their most familiar sound is the whinny, or neigh. Whinnies can be heard half a mile away. Horses use them for long-distance communication. Each horse has its own distinctive neigh, which its friends and family can recognize.

When a wild horse detects danger, it snorts a warning to members of its band. A snort from a band member will bring all heads up from grazing. The animals will look in the same direction, ready to flee.

The ears of a horse are a good indicator of its mood. When a horse is dozing, its ears flop to the sides with their openings downward. If a horse that isn't sleeping holds its ears this way, it may be very tired or ill. A horse often droops its ears as a sign of giving in to another horse that is trying to dominate it.

When a horse is feeling aggressive, it lays its ears flat against its head. When a horse lays its ears back, don't reach out toward its head — it might bite. Pulling its ears back can also be a sign that the horse senses it is in danger.

While horses' faces aren't as expressive as people's, you can still tell a great deal about how a horse is feeling from its mouth and eyes. Frightened or aggressive horses may raise their heads up and roll their eyes so that the white part shows. Pulled-back lips that reveal teeth mean they're threatening to bite. But if a young horse pulls back its lips and brings its teeth together, it means the horse is submitting (*giving in*) to another animal.

The tail can also reveal quite a bit about an animal's mood. Most often, the tail hangs down in a relaxed way or is used to swish away insects. But if a horse is tense or angry, it elevates the base of the tail so that it sticks out away from the body. If the horse begins to flick its tail back and forth, it may be ready to kick. A horse turning its backside toward you may also be warning that it is about to kick.

Unlawful to Photocopy

COMPARING LINKED PASSAGES

Now that you have read *Killer* and *How Horses Communicate*, let's look at the four questions you should think about when reading linked passages.

WHAT TYPE OF READING IS EACH PASSAGE?

KILLER
Short Story

HOW HORSES COMMUNICATE
Informational Reading

WHAT ARE THE MAIN IDEAS OR THEMES OF EACH READING?

★ **Killer** is story about a horse that is blamed for a boy's death ten years earlier. The horse is abandoned, but the boy telling the story shows kindness to the horse to gain its confidence. One day the horse becomes tangled on barbed wire. The boy tries to free it. Because the horse is familiar with the young boy, it does not try to kick him or go wild. Important themes of the story are kindness, communication between animals and humans, and having a second chance in life.

★ **How Horses Communicate** is an informational reading about how horses uses various sounds and body movements to communicate with one another and with people. Each gesture has a special meaning.

WHAT DO THE TWO PASSAGES HAVE IN COMMON?

UNLAWFUL TO PHOTOCOPY

In this case, both readings deal with the subject of horses. *How Horses Communicate* explains the different sounds and gestures that are made by horses. In *Killer*, the horse uses some of these gestures to communicate with the narrator.

HOW DO THE TWO READINGS DIFFER?

The two readings differ in some important ways. *Killer* is a short story. Like most short stories, it has a setting, characters, and plot. It has several themes, such as the need to treat animals with kindness and the importance of giving an animal or person a second chance in life.

How Horses Communicate is a short article. Its purpose is to inform the reader. It describes the sounds and gestures used by horses to communicate their feelings. The article explains what each sound or gesture means.

SHORT-RESPONSE QUESTIONS

Now that you have compared these linked passages, you are ready to tackle the kinds of questions that might appear on the test. Answer the three short-response questions below. They are similar to those questions you will find on **Session 3** of the actual test. Remember that you can look over the readings to help you answer each question.

1 Fill in the chart to show how horses communicate.

Horse Gestures	What it Means
Drooping ears	
Pulled-back lips	
Flicking tail	

2 What does it mean when the boy in the story whistles? Use details from the story to support your answer.

_____

_____

_____

Unlawful to Photocopy

3 Why does the boy prefer to call the horse "Champion" instead of "Killer"? Use details from the story to support your answer.

_____
_____
_____
_____

To answer these questions, take the same steps you learned for answering short-response questions in Chapter 11.

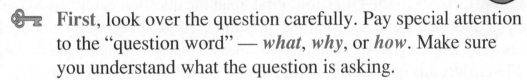

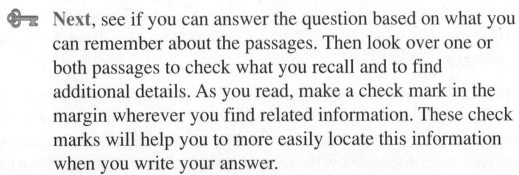

UNLOCKING THE ANSWER

First, look over the question carefully. Pay special attention to the "question word" — *what*, *why*, or *how*. Make sure you understand what the question is asking.

Next, see if you can answer the question based on what you can remember about the passages. Then look over one or both passages to check what you recall and to find additional details. As you read, make a check mark in the margin wherever you find related information. These check marks will help you to more easily locate this information when you write your answer.

Finally, write your answer clearly and neatly in the space provided. Be sure you answer the question. Before you have completed your answer it is always helpful to ask yourself: *Is my answer based on supporting details found in one or both of the reading passages?*

UNLAWFUL TO PHOTOCOPY

EXTENDED-RESPONSE QUESTIONS

Now let's look at an extended-response question based on the same two reading passages.

The extended-response question in **Session 3** will usually require you to use information from both readings. This is where you will need to make connections between the two passages.

> **4** How does the horse in the story communicate its feelings to the boy? In your answer, use details from both readings to describe the ways horses communicate and the ways in which the horse communicates in the story.

To answer this question, take the same steps you learned in Chapter 12 for answering other extended-response questions. Let's briefly review those steps:

★ **Step 1. Analyze the Question.** First, read the question carefully. Make sure you understand exactly what the question asks for. In question 4 above, you have to answer a *how* question: *how does the horse communicate to the boy?* To answer this question, you need to explain the meaning of some of the gestures used by the horse in the story to communicate. Remember that in **Session 3**, it will often be important to use information from *both* reading passages.

★ **Step 2. Plan Your Answer.** Now you are ready to plan your answer. Think about the two readings and what you should write. Then scan the two reading passages for helpful information. Place a check mark in the margin next to each description of how the horse communicates in the story. Then look in the article for places where that kind of horse gesture is described. This will provide you with the supporting details you need for your response.

For example, you might note that in the story the horse bends its neck towards the boy. Later, its ears flicker and its tail sticks out when it is caught in the barbed wire. The meaning of these gestures is explained in the article.

Based on the information you gather, it may help to create a short list of points you can use to answer the question:

UNLAWFUL TO PHOTOCOPY

Gesture in *Killer*	Meaning of Gesture in *How Horses Communicate*
Tail sticks out	A sign of tension or anger.

Once you have listed all your ideas and supporting details, you have to organize them to write your response. You might organize your ideas in the form of a "hamburger" or some other prewriting plan. Remember that your introduction should state the focus of your answer. It should be based on the question. For the body of your answer, write down your points and supporting details in some logical order. Here, you might use *time order*. State each gesture in the order that it happens in the story. Then explain what it means.

★ **Step 3. Write Your Answer.** Now simply turn your plan into your written answer. Make sure you use information from **both** passages in your response. Use colorful and precise words, including energetic, active verbs. Avoid vague or confusing sentences. Keep your writing natural. Do not try to impress the reader with words that you do not know how to use.

★ **Step 4. Revise Your Answer.** Read over your response before you hand it in. Make sure that your response stays focused on answering the question. Add anything you may have left out, and take out whatever you feel does not belong. Be sure to ask yourself a final time:

*Have I really explained how the
horse in the story communicates its feelings to the boy?*

Be sure you have included all of your best ideas. Give your final response a neat appearance that is easy to read. Use a margin on both sides of the paper. Begin each paragraph on a new line. Indent each new paragraph.

UNLAWFUL TO PHOTOCOPY

A MODEL EXTENDED-RESPONSE ANSWER

Look at the following student response to the extended-response question on page 154:

Notice how the introduction echoes the question and sets the focus.

> In *Killer*, the horse communicates its feelings to the boy through its movements and expressions. "How Horses Communicate" helps explain what many of these horse gestures mean.

This student has organized the response in time order. Note the transitions.

> At the beginning of the story, the horse bends its neck towards the boy but does not move. The boy does not know that Killer is trapped by barbed wire.

> The next day on his way home from school, the boy passes the horse again. This time he sees that the horse's tail is sticking out and the horse is making a snorting sound. From the article, we know these are signs of anger. When the boy helps the horse out of the barbed wire, the horse's eyes roll. From the article, we know the horse is frightened.

After describing each gesture in the story, the student then explains it.

> Finally, the horse is freed. Rather than run away from the boy, the horse calmly walks beside him. The horse blows on him and sniffs his chest. These are signs from the horse of friendship and happiness.

Notice how the conclusion restates the question in the form of a statement.

> From the two readings, we can see that the horse communicates to the boy in a number of ways. These gestures and sounds show many kinds of feelings — from fear to friendship.

UNLAWFUL TO PHOTOCOPY

PRACTICE EXERCISE

In this chapter, you have learned how to write an answer to an extended-response question in **Session 3**. Now it's your turn. Try answering the following question using the same paired readings you read in this chapter.

> **How do the story and article show that horses and people are similar in some ways? In your answer, use details from both reading passages.**

Use the space below to plan your answer:

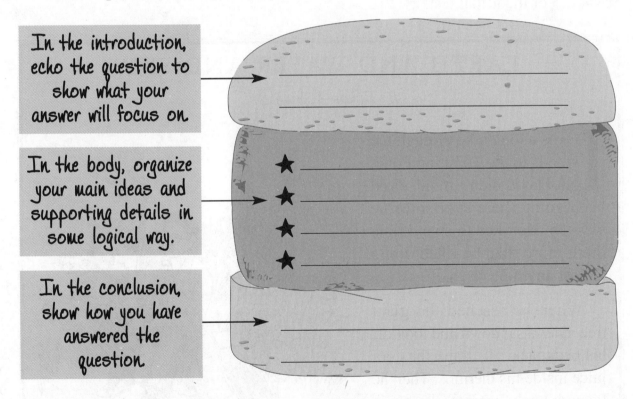

In the introduction, echo the question to show what your answer will focus on.

In the body, organize your main ideas and supporting details in some logical way.

In the conclusion, show how you have answered the question

Use a separate sheet of paper to write your answer.
After you complete your final draft, read over your response
one last time. Look for anything you might have missed.

UNLAWFUL TO PHOTOCOPY

CHAPTER 15

SESSION 3: PRACTICE ANSWERING LINKED PASSAGES

In this chapter, you will practice your new skills by answering three short-response and one extended-response question on two linked passages — just as you will on **Session 3** of the actual test.

EARTH AND WATER AND SKY

By Bryan A. Bushemi

It was a long hike through the woods to the Thinking Pond, but David didn't mind. He'd been going there ever since he was ten. He liked to spend time there more than he liked doing almost anything else.

When he reached the giant tree, David sat down and took off his backpack. He drank the cool juice inside his thermos. Then he leaned back against the wide trunk to rest for a few minutes.

Today David planned to sketch some fallen trees near the Thinking Pond. He liked to take his drawings back and have his dad scan them onto a disk. David would then color them on his computer. He had made some really cool prints that way.

CONTINUED ➡

UNLAWFUL TO PHOTOCOPY

David stood up and continued toward the Thinking Pond. Suddenly, he heard a sharp, whining sound like the engine of a high flying jet airplane.

It was followed by a *crack*! Like a whip being snapped, only a thousand times louder. Then a ball of fire roared overhead followed by a burning gust of wind. The shock wave knocked David to the ground, his ears ringing. A second later, he heard an explosive, hissing crash. He covered his head as a rush of air and hot steam rose through the trees.

After several minutes, David looked up. The warm, wet mist had disappeared, leaving the woods damp and sparkling with little droplets of water. *What the heck just happened*? he wondered as he got to his feet. Cautiously but curiously, he headed toward the Thinking Pond. By now David could usually see the shine of sunlight on the water, but today something was different. Covering the last yards quickly, David stopped at the edge of the meadow where the pond lay.

"Whoa!" he said in amazement.

Before him stretched a dry, cracked-mud crater, all that was left of the Thinking Pond. The water in the fifty-foot diameter pool had evaporated, leaving a huge hole in the forest floor. The baked mud rippled out from the center in wide, shallow waves. In the middle of the crater, half-buried in the ground, was a rounded, melted lump that looked like rock. It was a little larger than a baseball.

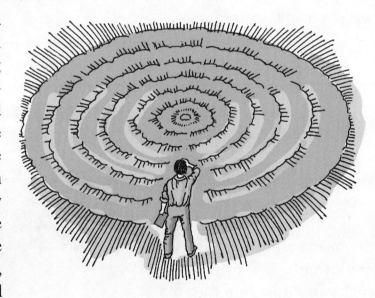

"I can't believe it!" David whispered, awe-struck. "It's a meteorite."

He stopped several feet away from the chunk of space rock, which was now giving off a faint sizzling noise. David picked up a small clump of mud oozing around his shoes. He flicked it onto the meteorite's rough surface. The wet dirt hissed and popped, then dried and stuck. The meteorite was definitely too hot to touch.

UNLAWFUL TO PHOTOCOPY

CONTINUED

While he waited for it to cool down, David took his sketch pad out of his backpack. With quick lines, he made a drawing of the rock. He made notes next to the drawing about shading and the faint rainbow tinting of the smoother parts.

Even as he was drawing, David could hardly believe he was looking at something that had been flying through space only minutes before.

He wondered where the meteorite had come from. Maybe an asteroid or a comet had passed too close to a planet or the Sun, and a chunk of it had been pulled off by gravity. Maybe it had been floating through space for millions of years before Earth's gravitational field caught it and dragged it in.

Danger From The Sky

by Barbara Saffer

A blazing streak shoots across the sky and drops to Earth with a loud boom, creating a noisy explosion. It throws rocks and dust into the air and cuts a large crater in the land. The collision causes earthquakes to erupt. Huge clouds of dust and steam surround the planet, blocking the

sun's light. Freezing darkness lasts for months, killing most plants and animals.

CONTINUED ➡

UNLAWFUL TO PHOTOCOPY

Many scientists believe this is exactly what happened about 65 million years ago. They think this is what probably caused the end of the dinosaurs.

But not all scientists agree. For years, scientists denied that there were any craters formed by meteors on Earth. A crater in Arizona was the first crater to be proven to have been caused by a meteor. Between 20,000 to 50,000  years ago, a small asteroid 80 feet in diameter hit the Earth and formed a crater over three miles across. The discovery of fragments of the meteorite* helped prove that this crater was in fact caused by the meteorite's impact.

Most objects from space usually don't crash into Earth. They merely dart across the sky, looking like streaks of light as they burn up in the atmosphere. These heavenly bodies are called meteors or shooting stars. Most are parts of large chunks of rocky material left from when the Sun and planets were formed.

Astronomers estimate that about 100,000 objects from space come near Earth each year and may threaten our planet. Meteoroids of all sizes regularly approach us. Most burn up as they race through the atmosphere. However, if a large meteor should survive its passage through the sky, it could cause great damage.

If a 600-foot-wide meteorite landed in the Pacific Ocean, it would create ocean waves large enough to destroy the coastal areas of Japan, China, Hawaii, and America's western shores. A similar impact in the Atlantic could destroy parts of Europe, Africa, and America's eastern shores. Even a small meteorite, say 30 feet wide, could destroy a city like Tokyo or Chicago.

***meteorite** = *a meteor that has entered the Earth's atmosphere.*

Unlawful to Photocopy

Based on the two passages you have just finished reading, answer the following questions:

1   What are some of the ways the meteorite is described in the story "Earth and Water and Sky"? Write your answer in the empty circles of the web below.

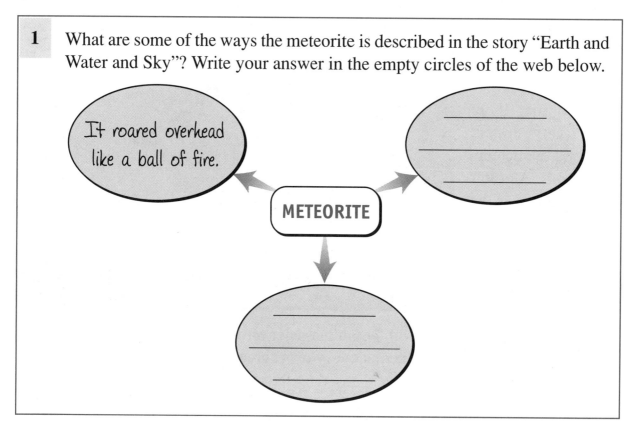

2   What effect does the meteorite have on the Thinking Pond? Use details from the story in your answer.

UNLAWFUL TO PHOTOCOPY

3 Why don't meteors cause even greater destruction on Earth? Use details from the article in your answer.

4 In the story, was David in any danger from the crash of the meteor? Use information from both the story and the article in your answer.

You may plan your answer in the box below if you wish.
Do not write your final answer here.

UNLAWFUL TO PHOTOCOPY

Now use a separate sheet of paper to write your final answer.

CHAPTER 16

A PRACTICE GRADE 4 ENGLISH LANGUAGE ARTS TEST

Now that you have mastered New York's Grade 4 English Language Arts standards, let's see how well prepared you are for the English Language Arts Test. Before you begin, take a moment to review what you will find on the test:

★ The test is divided into three sessions. Today you will take **Session 1**. Tomorrow you will take **Session 2.** On the third day you will take **Session 3**.

★ **Session 1** of the test consists of 28 multiple-choice questions. You will have **45 minutes** to complete **Session 1**. Read each selection carefully. Then answer the questions that follow it.

★ When you see the word **STOP** at the bottom of the page, you have finished the session. You may go back and check your work for that session only. Do not go on to the next day's session.

★ Once you finish checking your work, please stop writing, sit quietly, and do not disturb other students.

★ You will have 45 minutes to complete **Session 2**, and 60 minutes to complete **Session 3**.

★ For **Session 2** and **Session 3**, you may print your answers or write in cursive. Be sure to write clearly and neatly.

Taking this practice Grade 4 English Language Arts Test will help you to identify areas where you might still need to improve. We recommend that you take this practice test with your class. It should be taken under test conditions in a quiet room without distractions.

Good luck on this practice test!

Unlawful to Photocopy

SESSION 1

Read the following passage. Then answer the questions that follow.

ABBY TAKES HER SHOT

By Susan M. Dyckman

A blast of the buzzer ended the game, and the Hawks had won another. Abby leaped from the bench. Her throat hurt from cheering. The Hawks were undefeated after thirteen games — the best record a Willow Grove school team had ever had. Not that Abby had contributed much. Her playing time totaled only ten minutes for the entire season. Her brother constantly teased her. "You're a cheerleader in a basketball uniform."

Abby felt Mom's eyes on her from the bleachers. Abby forced a wave. At the meeting after the game, Coach McKenzie said, "Girls, your defense was awesome. And Kathy, your free-throw shooting helped a lot."

Abby felt like shouting, "My free-throw shooting could help — if I could just get in the game!" She thought of the hours she'd spent practicing. Abby was a fifth-grader and she'd made the team. But Abby learned that making the team and playing in games were two different things.

Mom was waiting in the car. Abby held back tears as she got in. "Are you OK?" Mom asked. Abby nodded. Mom always knew when to say something.

Suppertime was quiet. Dad had taken her brother to a scout meeting, so Abby was spared more teasing. After supper, Abby grabbed a basketball and raced downstairs. Mom came up behind her. "Want some company?" she asked.

"I guess," Abby answered. Mom took her spot under the basket.

UNLAWFUL TO PHOTOCOPY

"I know what you're going to say," Abby began. "I made the team and I should be happy."

Mom passed the ball back, and Abby took a jump shot . "I just want to say that I'm so proud of you for hanging in there," Mom replied.

Abby held the ball tightly and looked at Mom. "I really thought I'd play more. Even in fifth grade."

"I know you did, honey." Mom put her arms around Abby and hugged her. "Your time will come."

The gym was packed for the last game of the season. The lead went back and forth. At halftime Coach McKenzie was encouraging. "Stick to your game. Don't shoot until you get an open shot."

Abby watched as the second half began. The score remained close, and the Hawks trailed by one point in the final minute.

A few seconds later, Kathy stole the ball and raced to the basket. As she went up for the shot, an opponent knocked her to the floor. Kathy didn't get up. Coach McKenzie checked her ankle. It was twisted. Slowly, Kathy was helped up and taken to the bench.

The referee came over to the bench, too. "Coach, you need a player at the free-throw line. She gets two shots."

Coach looked at the players on the bench. She'd always stressed the importance of free-throw shooting. Who had paid attention? Abby. She hadn't played much, but she could shoot. "Abby," Coach said. "You're in."

Abby's stomach flipped. "Me?" she said. "Now?"

Coach leaned closer to her. "I've watched you in practice," she said. "You can do this." Abby walked to the foul line and glanced up at the scoreboard. Two points and a few seconds of defense would win the game.

UNLAWFUL TO PHOTOCOPY

The referee handed Abby the ball. She took a deep breath. Two bounces. She crouched and let the ball fly.

Swish went the basketball as it entered the hoop. The crowd roared. "One more," Abby thought. She caught the ball. Bounce, bounce. Shoot. The gym exploded with cheers as the ball went in a second time. Seconds later the buzzer sounded. The Hawks won and Abby's time had finally come.

1 Read this sentence from the story.

> **Dad had taken her brother to a scout meeting, so Abby was spared more teasing.**

The word "spared" means

A   given to

B   deserving of

C   helped with

D   saved from

2 What is the main problem of the story?

A   Abby is afraid Coach McKenzie will ask her to leave the team.

B   Abby is upset that she does not often play in team games.

C   Abby's brother teases her too much.

D   Abby wants to be as good a basketball player as Kathy.

3 Which of these best describes Abby's feelings when she goes into her mother's car?

A   Abby is unhappy to be leaving her friends and going home.

B   Abby is jealous of Kathy's talent for free-throw shooting.

C   Abby is upset that she has not played more this season.

D   Abby is angry at the way Coach McKenzie prepares the team.

4 Why is Abby's mother especially proud of Abby?

A   Abby helped clear the table after dinner.

B   Abby had made the school basketball team.

C   Abby was a good team player even when sitting on the bench.

D   Abby was a good free-throw shooter.

UNLAWFUL TO PHOTOCOPY

5 Why doesn't Coach McKenzie let Abby play in games more often?

A   She does not think Abby deserves to be on the team.
B   Kathy and Abby are too competitive on the court.
C   She is saving Abby for the most difficult plays.
D   She thinks the other girls are better players.

6 Which pair of words best describes Abby's mother?

A   supportive and helpful
B   competitive and funny
C   bossy and interfering
D   jealous and suspicious

7 The chart below shows the order in which some events happened in the story.

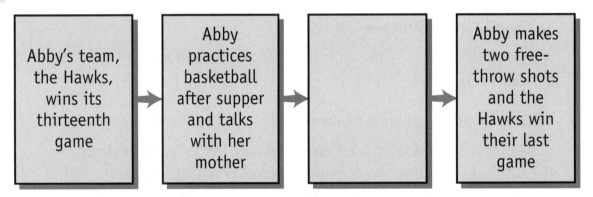

Abby's team, the Hawks, wins its thirteenth game → Abby practices basketball after supper and talks with her mother → [ ] → Abby makes two free-throw shots and the Hawks win their last game

Which of these sentences belongs in the empty box?

A   Abby's father takes her brother to a scout meeting.
B   Abby waves to her mother on the bleachers.
C   Kathy hurts her ankle and is forced to the bench.
D   The buzzer sounds, ending the game.

8 What lesson does Abby learn in the story?

A   Patience sometimes brings rewards.
B   Well trained athletes rarely get injured.
C   Having talent is more important than practicing.
D   Coaches do not always treat their players fairly.

UNLAWFUL TO PHOTOCOPY

CITY, CITY

by Marci Ridlon

I

City, city
Wrong and bad,
Looms* above me
When I'm sad,
Throws its shadow
On my care,
Sheds* its poison
In my air,
Pounds me with its
Noisy fist,
Sprays me with its
Sooty mist.
Till, with sadness
On my face,
I long to live
Another place.

II

City, city,
Golden-clad,*
Shines around me
When I'm glad,*
Lifts me with its
Strength and height,
Fills me with its
Sound and sight,
Takes me to its
Crowded heart,
Holds me so I
Won't depart.*
Till, with gladness
On my face,
I wouldn't live
Another place.

* **looms** = rises or towers above
* **sheds** = gives off

* **golden-clad** = dressed in gold
* **depart** = leave

9 What is the poem mostly about?

   A the good and bad sides of city life

   B the causes of pollution in the city

   C things that make the poet angry

   D the joys of moving to the countryside

10 What does the poet mean in the tenth line of the poem by "noisy fist"?

   A an automobile crash

   B a fight among city people

   C the loud noises of city life

   D the sounds of people arguing

UNLAWFUL TO PHOTOCOPY

11 When the poet is sad, the city

    A "looms above her"
    B "shines around her"
    C "takes her to its heart"
    D "holds her so she won't depart"

12 Based on the poem, which phrase best fits in the empty box below?

    A calm and silent
    B green and fresh
    C sound and sight
    D weak and hungry

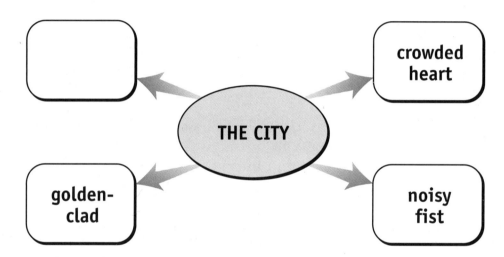

13 Which statement best expresses the poet's views?

    A The poet plans to leave the city because of its noise, dirt, and pollution.
    B The city fills the poet with strength when she is sad.
    C The city shines with gold, but she wants to live elsewhere.
    D The poet hates the city when she is sad, but loves the city when she is glad.

UNLAWFUL TO PHOTOCOPY

ALVIN AILEY

by Andrea Davis Pinkney

Alvin Ailey was born in 1931 in Rogers, Texas. As a young boy, he grew up in Navasota, Texas, where he regularly attended church with his mother. His memories of stomping feet, clapping hands, and singing along with the church choir inspired young Alvin to want to study dance.

As a young man, Alvin moved to New York City so he could study under the great dance masters. With a satchel hanging heavy on his shoulder, his shoes rapped a beat on the sidewalk while taxicabs honked their horns.

Alvin Ailey

He was glad to be in New York. He took dance classes all over town. At these classes, Alvin met dancers who showed him moves he'd never seen before. So many of the dancers he met were black. Like Alvin, their dreams soared higher than New York's tallest skyscrapers.

In the late 1950s, Alvin gathered some of the dancers he'd seen in classes around the city. He chose the men and women who had just the right moves to dance to his choreography. Alvin told them he wanted to start a modern dance company that would dance to blues and gospel music — the heritage of African American people. Nine dancers believed in Alvin's idea. This was the beginning of the Alvin Ailey American Dance Theatre.

On March 30, 1958, on an old wooden stage at the 92nd Street Y, Alvin and his friends opened for the first time with *Blues Suite*, dances set in a honky-tonk dance hall.

Alvin's choreography depicted the blues, that weepy sadness all folks feel now and then. Alvin moved in time to the music, the same way he did when he was a boy. The audience swayed in their seats as Alvin and his company danced. When the show ended, the audience went wild with applause. They stomped and shouted. "More!"

UNLAWFUL TO PHOTOCOPY

Taking a bow, Alvin let out a breath. He raised his eyes toward heaven, satisfied and proud. Alvin was on his way to making it big.

Word spread about him and his dancers. Newspapers hailed him. Under his leadership, the Alvin Ailey American Dance Theatre went on to receive international acclaim.

Corbis-Bettman Archives

Alvin Ailey gives instructions to some student dancers.

14 What is the article mostly about?

   A A young African American studies dance in Texas.

   B Alvin Ailey learns to dance with grace in New York City.

   C Alvin Ailey studies dance and forms a new dance company celebrating his African-American heritage.

   D Alvin Ailey's *Blues Suite* opens on March 30, 1958 at the 92nd Street YMCA.

15 Read this sentence from the article.

> **He chose men and women who had just the right moves to dance to his choreography.**

A "choreographer" is a person who

   A sings songs

   B writes music

   C creates dance steps

   D teaches in a school

UNLAWFUL TO PHOTOCOPY

16 Alvin learned from other dancers in New York how to

A   move to gospel music   C   play the piano
B   dance in new ways   D   read and write music

17 What words might be used to describe the "blues"?

A   teary and sadness
B   funny and festive
C   cheerful and peaceful
D   relaxed and carefree

18 The audience "stomped and shouted" at the 92nd Street Y because they

A   enjoyed Alvin and his dance company
B   were angry at the conditions of the theatre
C   were close friends of Alvin Ailey
D   wanted their money back after the performance

19 Which best describes the author's point of view?

A   The author does not like Alvin Ailey very much.
B   The author admires and respects Ailey's accomplishments.
C   The author feels that Ailey is a show-off.
D   The author believes that Ailey is the world's best dancer.

20 From information in the article, the reader could **best** conclude that

A   the audience at the 92nd Street Y did not really enjoy *Blues Suite*
B   Ailey's childhood experiences influenced his style of dancing
C   Ailey learned more about dancing in Texas than in New York
D   Ailey disliked dancing in front of large groups

UNLAWFUL TO PHOTOCOPY

HARD-BOILED EGGS

A Tale from Hungary Retold by Tom Kovach

In the kingdom of Hungary there once lived a man named Janos Kadar. After years of hard work, Janos was able to pay off all his debts and have enough money left to live comfortably. So one sunny morning he set out to repay a kind innkeeper who had once helped Janos when he was poor and hungry.

This innkeeper was surprised to see Janos. "Good day to you," said Janos. "Ten years ago you gave me two boiled eggs when I was hungry and had no money. Today, I want to reward your kindness by paying for those eggs a hundredfold!"

But the ten years had changed the innkeeper from a generous man to a greedy one. He began figuring what would have happened had the two eggs hatched chicks, and had those chicks grown up and hatched more chicks, and so on. He finally concluded that Janos should give him everything he had.

Janos was surprised and upset that his kind gesture should be met with such greedy demands. The news of this soon spread throughout the land. One day the King of Hungary himself heard the story and agreed to sit in judgment of what should be done.

CONTINUED ➔

As the time drew near for Janos and the innkeeper to present their cases, poor Janos grew sad. He felt his hard-earned savings would be lost, for the king would surely decide in favor of the innkeeper.

One day, as he sat thinking about his bad luck, a traveling gypsy came by [*gypsies were a wandering people*].

"Why are you so sad?" the gypsy asked. When Janos explained, the gypsy laughed. "You needn't worry. Let me present your case to the king, and you'll surely win." Although Janos had little hope, he agreed to let the gypsy try.

The day of the trial finally arrived, but when Janos reached the king's chamber, the gypsy was nowhere to be found. Everybody sat waiting, until finally the king grew impatient. "Janos Kadar," he said, "if the man representing you doesn't arrive in one minute, you'll have to pay the innkeeper all he asks for."

Just at that moment, the gypsy burst through the door. "I'm sorry for being late, Your Majesty," he said breathlessly, "but I was at home boiling corn, trying to turn it into more corn!"

Everyone in the king's chamber laughed. "You silly man," said the king, "how can you make more corn from boiled corn?"

The gypsy smiled. "Well then, Your Majesty, how can you hatch chicks from boiled eggs?"

"You're right," the king said. "If the eggs were boiled, it would be impossible to hatch chicks. Janos, pay only for the two eggs you ate."

Janos thanked the king and gypsy traveler, paid the innkeeper and went home happy.

As for the innkeeper, because of his greed he only got paid for the two eggs, instead of the reward Janos had first offered him.

UNLAWFUL TO PHOTOCOPY

21 What is the main idea of the story?

   A Chicks cannot be hatched from boiled eggs.

   B A greedy person may take advantage of a kindness if not prevented.

   C Kings in former times were often unfair in their judgments.

   D Repaying borrowed money is an important responsibility.

22 Read this sentence from the story.

> **Janos was surprised and upset that his kind gesture should be met with such greedy demands.**

In this sentence, "gesture" means

   A a movement of the head

   B a pointing of the hand

   C an action showing feeling

   D a joke or humorous story

23 What is the main problem that Janos faces in the story?

   A Janos refuses to pay the innkeeper what he owes.

   B The innkeeper tries to take Janos' savings with a false claim.

   C The innkeeper needs money for his family to live comfortably.

   D The gypsy is in need of more corn.

24 Which pair of words best describes the gypsy?

   A greedy and selfish

   B fair and generous

   C kind but foolish

   D light-hearted but clever

25 What is the best reply that the innkeeper might have given to the gypsy?

   A If Janos hadn't come to his inn, he never would have boiled the eggs.

   B Boiled eggs might still hatch some chicks.

   C Janos owed him the money anyway.

   D The gypsy had no right to interfere in the dispute.

UNLAWFUL TO PHOTOCOPY

A bowl of McAllen's Oats is the best tasting cereal on the planet!

No other cereal tastes quite so delicious as McAllen's Oats. Many people enjoy eating our cereal with brown sugar and milk. Others eat it with berries, bananas, and other fruits.

Recent studies have shown that oatmeal is good for your health. In one study, people who ate oats each morning for two months lowered their cholesterol levels up to 20%!

So, what are you waiting for? Try McAllen's Oats today!

26 The main purpose of this advertisement is to

   A tell an interesting story

   B inform readers about a recent medical study

   C persuade readers to buy McAllen's Oats

   D explain the importance of eating a healthy breakfast

27 Which statement from the advertisment expresses an opinion?

   A "No other cereal tastes quite as delicious as McAllen's Oats."

   B "Many people enjoy eating our cereal with brown sugar and milk."

   C "Recent studies have shown that oatmeal is good for your health."

   D "In one study, people who ate oats each morning for two months lowered their cholesterol levels up to 20%!"

28 In what way is this advertisement biased?

   A It reports the results of a scientific study.

   B It only tells the advantages of eating McAllen's Oats.

   C It tells what people eat with McAllen's Oats.

   D It includes a picture of a bowl of McAllen's Oats with fruit.

UNLAWFUL TO PHOTOCOPY

SESSION 2

Your teacher will read a story two times. Listen carefully each time the story is read. You may take notes while listening. Then answer the questions below.

29 In the chart below, write two things describing how each animal lives.

Description	The Dog	The Wolf
Where they live		
How they get food		

30 What things does the dog promise if the wolf goes home with him?

_____

_____

_____

_____

_____

31 Why does the wolf decide to run away? Use details from the story to support your answer.

> *You may plan your answer in the box below if you wish.*

Now use a separate sheet of paper to write your final answer.

UNLAWFUL TO PHOTOCOPY

STOP

SESSION 3

Read the two passages and then answer the questions that follow.

INTO THE CAVE

By Harriet Diller and Betty Hodges

Standing outside the cave entrance, Grandfather admired the green hills of Guilin. "Next to heaven," he said, "Guilin is most beautiful."

And I would rather be anywhere else in China, Lin thought. He had come here today only because of Grandfather, who refused to use anything but guano[1] to fertilize his crops. Grandfather used to come here by himself. But lately he was too weak. He would gather the guano and bring it out of the cave in a red basket, but he needed Lin to haul it home in the wooden cart.

Grandfather took a shovel and flashlight from the cart. "Come inside with me?" he asked. Lin had not been in the cave for months. Not since the Terrible Day of the Bats.

"It won't happen again, Lin," Grandfather promised. "That other time was my mistake. I waited until dusk to go inside. I know the bats fly out of the cave at dusk.[2]" As Lin had stood at the cave entrance, a swarm of black bats had erupted from it. Lin had been terrified.

"Bats hurt no one," Grandfather said. "Besides, you startled them as much as they did you." Nothing could make Lin forget the horror he felt enclosed in a cloud of bats. "I can't go in there," he told Grandfather.

---

[1]guano is the manure, or waste matter, of bats, often used as fertilizer.
[2]dusk is the time of day when the sun is setting.

UNLAWFUL TO PHOTOCOPY

"OK," Grandfather said. He started into the cave still speaking, "I'll be out in no time."

Lin walked down to the river. Grandfather would call when he was finished. Lin watched as two little children splashed about at the edge of the river. Then Lin realized that Grandfather's "no time" had turned into a long time. Had he hauled the cart home by himself? Lin hurried toward the cave. The cart was there. Grandfather was still inside. Something had gone wrong.

Lin peered into the darkness. *I can't go in there*, he thought. Then he imagined Grandfather hurt and alone. Sweating, Lin reached for his flashlight. Go, he urged himself. *You're the only one who can help.*

Lin took a deep breath and started into the cave. He turned on the flashlight. Evil faces seemed to peer at him from the darkness. *Drip, plink, plop.* Lin had forgotten about the sounds in the cave. Dripping water. Then he heard a flittering noise. A bat? Lin swung the flashlight around and saw the creature. Just a bird. As Lin started through a narrow passage, something scurried away from him. *Probably just a mouse*, he thought. His hand was shaking.

"Grandfather!" Lin yelled. The darkness exploded. Bats. Thousands of them. Maybe millions. Lin shuddered as he covered his face with his arms. It was the Terrible Day of the Bats all over again.

As he huddled there, Lin remembered Grandfather's words. *Bats hurt no one. You startled them as much as they did you.* Lin gathered his courage. Then he yelled again, "Grandfather." Through the flittering and whirling of wings, he heard an answer. Lin pushed farther into the cave. "Grandfather!"

"Over here." In a moment Lin was at Grandfather's side. "Slipped and twisted my knee," Grandfather said. "Can you —"

"Here, Grandfather," said Lin. "Lean on me."

UNLAWFUL TO PHOTOCOPY

The bats had begun to calm down now. Slowly, Lin helped Grandfather back to the cave entrance. Grandfather would be OK. While Grandfather waited, Lin went back into the cave and got Grandfather's flashlight, shovel, and guano-filled basket.

Outside, Lin stood for a moment with Grandfather, looking out at the hills of Guilin. He glanced back at the black mouth of the cave. "You were right, Grandfather," Lin said. "Guilin is most beautiful."

Batty About BATS!

by Kathiann M. Kowalski

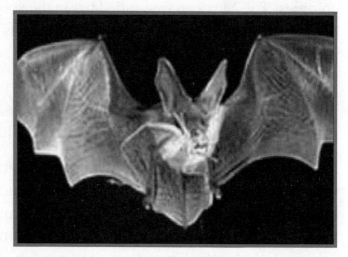

Don't you hate it when a mosquito buzzes around your head when you're trying to sleep? Bzzzzzz. . . Or when the pesky critters join your camp-out, leaving your body with itchy lumps? Imagine what it would be like if there were millions more mosquitoes! Or, worse yet, what if the insects that eat farmers' crops multiplied by the millions? Do you like bats? Well, without them, these two scenarios would become reality. Whether you like them or not, we need bats.

FLYING

Bats are the only true flying mammals. Thin membranes sandwich muscles and blood vessels, and connect a bat's arm, palm, and finger bones to its ankles — forming wings. Because wings are crucial for flying and feeding, bats spend lots of time grooming them.

FEEDING

Flying takes lots of energy, so bats eat about half their weight in food each day. What's on the menu? It depends. "Bats fill every conceivable feeding niche," says Ken Paige at the University of Illinois. Over 200 of the 925 known species eat fruits or flower nectar. Other bat species eat mosquitoes, flies, moths, beetles, or termites. Still others feed on frogs, fish, lizards, or other animals. Bats generally pose no threat at all to humans.

UNLAWFUL TO PHOTOCOPY

When food gets scarce in areas outside the tropics, some bat species migrate[1]. Others hibernate[2] through the cold winter.

HANGING OUT

Bats roost by hanging upside down. Their small size keeps all the blood from rushing to their heads. Where bats roost varies from species to species. Some choose old trees, buildings, or attics. Others build tents from leaves.

Other species haunt caves in giant colonies. The Mexican free-tailed bat in the southwestern United States forms one of the largest groups of mammals, with millions of bats per cave. So many bats may seem scary to cave visitors, but cave bats are completely harmless to humans.

SUPER SONAR

How do bats get around in the dark? No, bats are not blind. They all can see. Some fruit-eating and nectar-drinking bats actually have excellent vision.

About 670 species — mostly those who eat moving animals — supplement their vision with *echolocation*. "They create maps of their environment by sound," explains Dean Waters at Great Britain's University of Leeds. The bats send out high-frequency cries above the range of human hearing. Then they interpret the echoes. Echolocation measures the time for echoes to bounce back. "Bats can not only range targets, but can also classify them depending on how they 'sound,'" says Waters.

Bats rely on other environmental clues, too. Insects are more likely to buzz about under certain air pressure conditions. By sensing pressure changes in the middle ear, bats know when they can find abundant food without spending unnecessary energy flying out to check.

---

[1]**migrate** means to move to warmer areas in winter
[2]**hibernate** means to go into a sleeplike state, some mammals hibernate during the winter months.

UNLAWFUL TO PHOTOCOPY

1 What happened to Lin on the "Terrible Day of the Bats"?

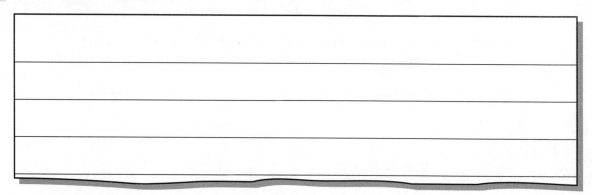

2 In the story, what prevented Grandfather from coming out of the cave "in no time"?

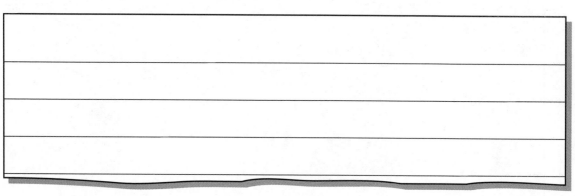

3 Complete the chart below by writing three facts about bats based on information from the article.

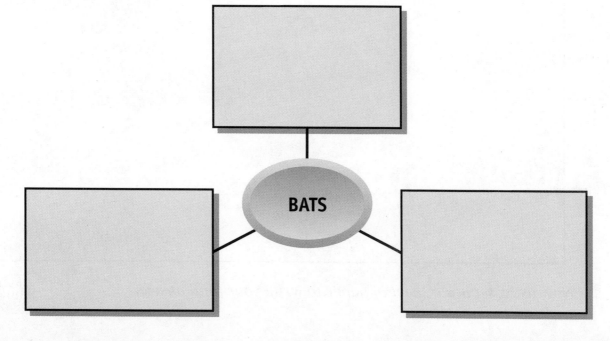

UNLAWFUL TO PHOTOCOPY

4 Explain why Lin had nothing to fear from the bats in the cave. Use information from both the story and article to support your answer.

You may plan your answer in the box below if you wish.
Do not write your final answer here.

Now use a separate sheet of paper to write your final answer

(STOP)

UNLAWFUL TO PHOTOCOPY

APPENDIX

WRITING MECHANICS

English has rules for standard spelling, capitalization, punctuation, and usage. Your extended responses will receive a separate score for how well you follow these rules. Students most often make mistakes in the following areas:

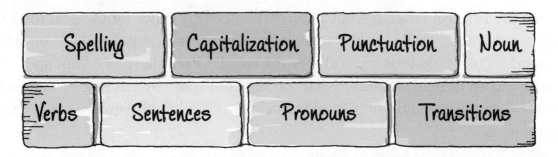

This appendix reviews each of these areas to help you avoid common mistakes.

SPELLING

RULE 1:

A **noun** is a word naming a person, place or thing. When a noun ends in *y* after a consonant, change the *y* to an *i* and add *es* to make it plural.

story	stories		city	cities

RULE 2:

A **verb** is an action word. When a noun ends in a consonant plus an *e*, drop the final *e* before adding *ing*.

hide	hiding		love	loving

UNLAWFUL TO PHOTOCOPY

RULE 3:

To spell words with *ei* or *ie,* use *i* before *e*, except after *c,* or when sounding like *ay,* as in *neighbor* or *weigh.*

p*ie*ce	ch*ie*f	c*ei*ling	sl*eigh*

There are a few important exceptions to the rule, such as:

w*ei*rd	s*ei*ze

RULE 4:

Because the English language has been influenced by other languages, the same sound is not always spelled in the same way. When you misspell a word or learn a new word, you should look carefully at the word. Often there is a "hot spot" that makes the word difficult to spell. Focus on the "hot spot" by circling it. Then write the word correctly several times from memory. Keep a list of words you have difficulty spelling.

CHECKING YOUR UNDERSTANDING

Circle the "hot spot" in each of the following words.

Tuesday	weather	balloon	swimming
their	friend	afraid	separate
receive	there	February	Wednesday

CAPITALIZATION

You should use the following rules for capitalization:

★ Always begin each sentence with a capital letter.

★ Always capitalize the pronoun *I.*

★ Proper nouns, such as *people's name*s, begin with capital letters.

★ *Mr., Mrs.* and *Ms.* are capitalized.

★ Days, months, holidays, book titles, streets, cities, and countries are proper nouns and begin with capital letters: *Monday, Thanksgiving, Albany, China*

Unlawful to Photocopy

CHECKING YOUR UNDERSTANDING

*Underline each letter of the following nouns
that should be capitalized.*

★ mr. smith

★ florida

★ bread

★ meat loaf

★ strawberry jam

★ disneyland

PUNCTUATION

Here are some rules you should know for punctuation:

★ Use **commas** to separate the items in a list, dates, quotations, and places in a sentence where you would pause. Also use commas to separate a city from its state or country:

> *Lenny brought tomatoes, eggs, milk, and a
> loaf of bread to his hotel room in Syracuse, New York.*

★ Use commas before *and*, *or*, and *but* in compound sentences:

> *Katy refused to listen, but I insisted that she leave.*

★ Use periods at the end of abbreviations: *Mr., Ms., Mrs., U.S.A.*

★ Use apostrophes to show possession or contractions:

> *Jack's boat   I'm = I am*

★ Use quotation marks for direct speech: *"I want to go home," she said*.

★ Always end a sentence with a period, question mark or exclamation point.

- End statement with a period: *The monkey ate a bunch of bananas.*

- End questions with a question mark: *What time is it?*

- End sentences that show strong feelings, such as surprise or laughter, with an exclamation point: *That hat looks silly on you*!

Unlawful to Photocopy

CHECKING YOUR UNDERSTANDING

Insert the correct punctuation in the following paragraph:

It was late at night on October 13 ⬚ 1995 ⬚ Everything was quiet in the house ⬚ Suddenly we heard a crash ⬚ A large number of people rushed out of their homes to see what was going on ⬚ ⬚ Is anyone hurt ⬚ ⬚ our neighbor asked ⬚ ⬚ It looks like there was an earthquake ⬚ ⬚ my mother answered ⬚

PRONOUNS

Pronouns take the place of nouns. Pronouns take different forms when they are used in different places in a sentence.

⭐ If the pronoun is the subject, use *I, you, he, she, it, we,* or *they.*

> **He** is going to karate class.

⭐ If the pronoun is not the subject of the sentence, use *me, you, him, her, it, us,* and *them.* These are known as **object pronouns**.

> Chinami gave **them** the present.
> Carson sent a birthday card to **her**.

CHECKING YOUR UNDERSTANDING

Select the correct pronoun to complete the following sentences:

1. (*He / Him*) went to the zoo for a visit.

2. (*She / Her*) baked (*he / him*) a cake for his birthday.

3. (*They / Them*) like to go bowling on Saturday.

UNLAWFUL TO PHOTOCOPY

Some pronouns raise special problems. Here are three groups that often cause confusion:

★ **It's / Its**

It's is a contraction for two words — *it* and *is*:

> **It's** time to go to bed.

Its without an apostrophe shows possession:

> The lost dog missed **its** owner.

★ **There / their / they're**

There means a place:

> He lives over **there**.

Their shows possession:

> **Their** car is waiting.

They're is a contraction for two words — *they are*:

> **They're** going away.

★ **Your / You're**

Your shows possession:

> Is this **your** boat?

You're means *you are*:

> **You're** in a good mood today.

CHECKING YOUR UNDERSTANDING

Select the correct form of the word to complete the following sentences:

1. (*Its* / *It's*) time for us to go home.

2. Are these (*your* / *you're*) hat and gloves?

3. The monster lives (*there* / *their* / *they're*).

UNLAWFUL TO PHOTOCOPY

VERBS

A **verb** gives the action of the sentence. Verbs take different forms, known as **tenses**, to tell us when the action takes place. Different tenses are used to express actions in the *present, past,* and *future.*

Past Tense	Present Tense	Future Tense
He liked her.	He likes her.	He will like her.
She was eating.	She is eating.	She will be eating.

When you write, be sure to keep your verbs in the right tense. If a story takes place in the past, keep all of the verbs you are using in the past tense. Change the tense of the verb only if the action moves to the present or future.

SENTENCES

A sentence is a group of words that expresses a complete thought. Every sentence has a **subject** — the person or thing that the sentence is about. The subject could be singular or plural. Each sentence also has a **predicate** — a verb that tells something about the subject. The verb could be an action that the subject does, an action that is done to the subject, or the subject's condition.

> *Jack and Jill went up the hill.*

Jack and Jill make up the subject of the sentence. The predicate is *went*. This word tells us what Jack and Jill did.

> *Jack was tired.*

Jack is the subject of this sentence. *Was* is the verb. It tells us Jack's condition. In this sentence, he was tired.

Unlawful to Photocopy

SENTENCE FRAGMENTS

If a sentence does not express a complete thought or is missing its subject or predicate, it is not a complete sentence but a **sentence fragment**. When you read a sentence fragment, you feel like part of the sentence is missing.

 Lacks a Complete Thought. Here are two examples of sentence fragments:

> *"When I was younger."*
> *"Going to baseball games with my family."*

 Has a Complete Thought. Here is an example of a complete sentence:

> *"When I was younger, I loved going to baseball games with my family."*

A **clause** is a group of words with a subject and predicate. Some clauses are sentences, but others are not. Clauses beginning with *after*, *until*, *because*, or *since* do not express a complete thought. The words introducing the clauses show a relationship. When these clauses stand alone, part of the relationship is missing.

For example, *"After I went shopping."* Here, the reader asks what happened *after* you went shopping. The clause does not have a complete thought. It needs to be joined to another clause telling what you did after shopping.

CHECKING YOUR UNDERSTANDING

Check (✔) the examples that are complete sentences.

❑ Before I went to bed.

❑ They listened to the radio.

❑ Since you left.

❑ He had eggs yesterday.

❑ Because she was hungry.

❑ I enjoy your company.

UNLAWFUL TO PHOTOCOPY

RUN-ON SENTENCES

The opposite of a sentence fragment is a run-on sentence. A **run-on sentence** usually occurs when the writer joins several separate sentences together by commas. For example:

> *"Nancy liked the summer, her father preferred the fall."*

There are several ways to correct a run-on sentence. One way is to divide it into two or more separate sentences. A second approach is to turn the run-on sentence into a *compound* or *complex* sentence by adding *conjunctions* or *relative pronouns*: *Nancy liked the summer,* ***while*** *her father preferred the fall."*

SUBJECT-VERB AGREEMENT

A very common mistake in sentences occurs in *subject / verb agreement*. The subject and verb (*predicate*) of the sentence must agree in number.

★ A **singular subject** refers to one person, place or thing. If the subject of a sentence is singular, you must use a verb in its **singular form**.

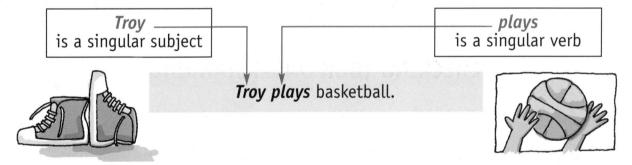

Troy
is a singular subject

plays
is a singular verb

Troy plays basketball.

★ A **plural subject** consists of more than one person, place, or thing. The subject may be a plural noun (*children*) or a compound subject (*John and Jack*). If the subject of a sentence is plural, the verb must be in its plural form.

Jack *likes* to drink water.
John and Jack *like* to drink water.
The children *like* to drink water.

UNLAWFUL TO PHOTOCOPY

SENTENCE PATTERNS

Good writers think about and vary their sentence patterns. They often use compound subjects and predicates, or compound and complex sentences:

★ **Compound Subjects and Predicates.** Some simple sentences have more than one subject or more than one verb.

> *Jack and Jill went up the hill.*
> *They fetched a pail of water and brought it down the hill.*

★ **Compound Sentences.** A compound sentence joins together two *independent sentences* with **and**, **or**, **but**, **yet**. Always put a comma before the conjunction to make a compound sentence.

> *Jack and Jill went up the hill, and Jill went to fetch a pail of water.*
> *Jack liked soda, but Jill preferred fruit juice.*

★ **Complex Sentences.** A complex sentence is made up of a main clause and one or more subordinate clauses. Subordinate clauses are introduced by words such as *because*, *as*, *while*, *since*, *which* or *that*:

> *Jack could not climb the hill because he was tired.*
> *This is the hill that Jack climbed.*

TRANSITIONS

Transitions words or phrases link together different ideas by telling the relationship between them. They act as signposts to readers, telling them they are entering a new area or topic in your writing. By using transitions, your writing will flow more smoothly.

UNLAWFUL TO PHOTOCOPY

★ **Time and Place.** Some transitions show there has been a change in time or place:

> *He ate dinner at 7 o'clock. Later that evening, he went to bed.*

While and *meanwhile* indicate a change of place at the same time.

> *Tom was working in Manhattan.*
> *Meanwhile, Cheryl was meeting friends in Albany.*

★ **New Points or Examples.** Transitions can be used to show you are moving from one point to the next.

> *A second reason for inspecting luggage at airports is to stop people from taking weapons on airplanes.*

★ **Introducing Differences.** Transitions often introduce something that is different from what has already been said. The words *however* and *although* mark a contrast or change in direction.

> *I enjoy jogging. However, in the summer heat I prefer to swim.*

★ **Conclusions.** Transitions can also be used to indicate a conclusion.

> *Therefore, he had no choice but to help his father.*

UNLAWFUL TO PHOTOCOPY

The EMPEROR AND THE BOY

There once lived an emperor who liked to disguise himself when traveling among his people, in order to learn their true opinions and feelings. One day, the emperor put on a disguise and went out into the countryside. During his travels, he came upon a poor, young boy gathering twigs for his family.

"You hardly have enough twigs to build a fire," the disguised emperor told the boy. "Why not collect more twigs from the royal forest across the road?" The boy, not realizing who this stranger really was, said, "Kind traveler, you are obviously not from this area. If you were, you would know the forest belongs to the emperor. It is forbidden for anyone to enter the royal forest."

"Surely," the emperor replied, "no one would know if you went there. Your emperor must be very cruel to allow twigs to lie in the forest while his subjects remain cold without a fire."

"I agree with you that the law is unjust," the boy said. "But the law is the law, and I will not disobey it." He then walked away, carrying his small bundle of twigs.

Two days later the young boy and his family were summoned to the emperor's palace. When they arrived, they were immediately brought before the emperor. The boy shuttered when he recognized that the traveler he had met a few days earlier was actually the royal emperor! He feared the emperor would punish him for speaking out against the emperor's law.

"Fear not," said the emperor calmly, "you've done nothing wrong. I just wanted to meet the parents who raised such an honest child." Just then, a servant entered the room with a trunk filled with gold. The emperor gave the family the trunk with its riches.

The emperor then said, "I have decided to change my law governing the royal forest. You were right, young man. The law is unjust. From now on, all my subjects can use the forest lands to meet their needs. All of this because your honesty has touched my heart."

UNLAWFUL TO PHOTOCOPY

THE SON AND THE THIEF

Long ago in ancient China, there lived a young man by the name of Li. He devoted himself to the task of caring for his old, widowed mother. Li cooked for her, and made sure she took her medicine every night. He brought old friends to see his mother so that she would not be lonely. And once a week, he took her to his father's resting place where she grieved quietly while Li swept the grave.

One evening a thief broke into their house. The thief made Li and his mother sit in the corner while he searched their home. He carried a cloth bag and began stuffing it with whatever he thought worth stealing.

The thief took Li's silk robe. This robe was the only piece of good clothing the young man owned. Li watched and said nothing. He took Li's jacket, the only one he had to keep warm on bitter cold mornings. Again, the youth kept silent. He took Li's jade ring, which Li's father had given to him. Although the young man's lip trembled, he still said nothing.

Then the thief reached for an old pot. "Please, be kind enough to leave us that old pot," Li said. "If you take it, I won't be able to make my mother's dinner."

The thief dropped the pot and looked in wonder at the young man and his mother. "Heaven will surely curse me if I rob a house where such a loyal and devoted son lives," he cried. The thief immediately emptied his bag of all he had stolen, and left with a softened heart.

Setting: A poor house in ancient China

Main Characters: ★ Li ★ His mother ★ The Thief

Problem Faced by Main Characters: Li and his mother are being robbed by a thief.

Main Story Events
★ Li — devoted son — lives with his mother.
★ A thief breaks in and begins stealing a robe, jacket, ring, and old pot
★ Li asks thief to keep pot used for his mother's food
★ Thief struck by Li's love of mother, leaves without taking anything

Other Information: A thief learns that some things in life are more £ important than expensive objects.

UNLAWFUL TO PHOTOCOPY